ICFA Continuing Education
Value and Growth Styles in Equity Investing

Proceedings of the AIMR seminar *Equity Investing: Value and Growth*

February 15, 1995
New York, New York

Stanford Calderwood
Charles D. Ellis, CFA, *moderator*
William C. Fletcher, CFA
J. Parker Hall III, CFA
James R. Jundt, CFA
Edward C. Mitchell, Jr., CFA

John B. Neff, CFA
Patrick O'Donnell
Claude N. Rosenberg, Jr.
Lewis A. Sanders, CFA
Warren E. Shaw, CFA

Edited by Jan R. Squires, CFA

To obtain an AIMR Publications Catalog or to order additional copies of this publication, turn to page 63 or contact:

AIMR
P.O. Box 3668
Charlottesville, VA 22903
U.S.A.
Telephone: (804) 980-3668
Fax: (804) 980-9755

The Association for Investment Management and Research comprises the Institute of Chartered Financial Analysts and the Financial Analysts Federation.

ICFA Continuing Education is published eight times a year by the Association for Investment Management and Research, P.O. Box 3668, Charlottesville, Virginia 22903. This publication is designed to provide accurate and authoritative information in regard to the subject matter covered. It is sold with the understanding that the publisher is not engaged in rendering legal, accounting, or other professional service. If legal advice or other expert assistance is required, the services of a competent professional should be sought. Application to mail at second class postage rates is pending at Charlottesville, Virginia, and additional mailing offices.

Copies are mailed as a benefit of membership to CFA® charterholders. Subscriptions also are available at $100 for one year. Address all circulation communications to ICFA Continuing Education, P.O. Box 3668, Charlottesville, Virginia 22903; (804) 980-3668; FAX (804) 980-9755. For change of address, send mailing label and new address six weeks in advance.

Postmaster: Send address changes to the Association for Investment Management and Research, P.O. Box 3668, Charlottesville, Virginia 22903.

ISBN 1-879087-54-5

Printed in the United States of America

September 1995

Contents

Foreword vii
   Katrina F. Sherrerd, CFA

Biographies of Speakers viii

Value and Growth in Equity Investing: An Overview 1
   Jan R. Squires, CFA

The Positive Bias for Value Investors in U.S. Equities 4
   Stanford Calderwood

Value Investing in a Style-Neutral World 14
   William C. Fletcher, CFA

Stock Valuation and Selection: A Value Investor's Perspective 21
   Edward C. Mitchell, Jr., CFA

The Advantage to Value Investing 28
   Lewis A. Sanders, CFA

Question and Answer Session: Value 35
   Stanford Calderwood
   William C. Fletcher, CFA
   Edward C. Mitchell, Jr., CFA
   Lewis A. Sanders, CFA

The Security Analyst's Changing Role 37
   Patrick O'Donnell

An Approach to Growth Investing 43
   J. Parker Hall III, CFA

A Unique Approach to Growth Investment Management 47
   James R. Jundt, CFA

Growth Stock Investing Today 51
   Claude N. Rosenberg, Jr.

Growth Investing: Earnings Momentum and Delivered Growth 55
   Warren E. Shaw, CFA

(continued on next page)

Question and Answer Session: Growth 62
    J. Parker Hall III, CFA
    James R. Jundt, CFA
    Claude N. Rosenberg, Jr.
    Warren E. Shaw, CFA

Order Form 63

Selected Publications 64

Foreword

Some 50 years ago, equity investment managers and analysts—in their never-ending search for an approach to investing that will enhance client returns and consistently beat the market (and competitors)—divided into two fundamental camps or styles. The division into those pursuing value versus those pursuing growth has dominated equity investing ever since. By now, we have had a fairly long time to fine-tune the most successful approaches within each style. We also have benchmarks defined by value or growth and a fairly long history of performance data. The conference on applying the value and growth styles to equity investing from which this proceedings developed sprang from the realization that now was a good time to review the state of the value–growth rivalry.

The conference provided an opportunity for participants to focus on the investment criteria and performance characteristics of each style. In addition, the conference raised some interesting questions about the appropriateness of viewing equity investing as divided along these style lines in the future. Readers will find in the proceedings the definitions of value and growth, philosophies, and strategies of well-known and highly skilled proponents of each style. The proceedings allows readers to assess the similarities and differences between the two approaches and among the approaches of practitioners. We are extremely pleased to offer readers this unique opportunity to learn the insights and advice on successful style implementation from these outstanding practitioners.

We would like to thank Charles D. Ellis, CFA, of Greenwich Associates for organizing and moderating the conference and Jan R. Squires, CFA, of Southwest Missouri State University for serving as editor of the proceedings and furnishing the overview. We would especially like to thank the conference speakers for sharing their wisdom and experience with us: Stanford Calderwood, Trinity Investment Management Corporation; William C. Fletcher, CFA, Independence Investment Associates; J. Parker Hall III, CFA, Lincoln Capital Management Company; James R. Jundt, CFA, Jundt Associates; Edward C. Mitchell, Jr., CFA, INVESCO Capital Management; John B. Neff, CFA, Wellington Management Company (who, unfortunately, was unable to prepare his presentation for publication in the proceedings); Patrick O'Donnell, Putnam Investments; Claude N. Rosenberg, Jr., RCM Capital Management; Lewis A. Sanders, CFA, Sanford C. Bernstein and Company; and Warren E. Shaw, CFA, Chancellor Capital Management.

Katrina F. Sherrerd, CFA
Senior Vice President
Education

Biographies of Speakers

Stanford Calderwood is chairman and CEO of Trinity Investment Management Corporation. Previously, he served as vice chairman of Endowment Management and Research, executive vice president and president of ten overseas subsidiaries of the Polaroid Corporation, and president of WGBH-TV in Boston, where he raised funds to launch *Masterpiece Theater* on the PBS network. Mr. Calderwood is a graduate of the University of Colorado.

Charles D. Ellis, CFA, is managing partner of Greenwich Associates. He has taught second-year investment management courses at Harvard Business School and the Yale School of Management and has served as a faculty member of AIMR's Investment Management Workshop for more than a decade. Dr. Ellis has authored numerous books and articles, including "The Loser's Game," which appeared in the *Financial Analysts Journal* in 1975 and for which he won the Graham & Dodd Award. He has served as a trustee of The Institute of Chartered Financial Analysts (ICFA), president of the ICFA, and the 1993–94 chair of AIMR. Dr. Ellis is an overseer of the School of Business at New York University and a member of the Yale University Investment Committee. He holds a B.A. from Yale University, an M.B.A. from Harvard Business School, and a Ph.D. from New York University.

William C. Fletcher, CFA, is president and chief investment officer of Independence Investment Associates, an investment management firm that manages approximately $15 billion in institutional stock and bond assets. Mr. Fletcher began his career in 1968 as an investment analyst with Brown Brothers Harriman Company in New York. In 1973, he joined John Hancock, where he served as a research director and portfolio manager. Mr. Fletcher holds a B.A. from Bowdoin College and an M.B.A. from the University of Michigan Graduate School of Business.

J. Parker Hall III, CFA, is president of Lincoln Capital Management Company, a position he has held for twenty years. He is a former president of the Investment Analysts Society of Chicago and currently serves on the board and the investment committee of the University of Chicago. Mr. Hall is the author of several articles that have appeared in the *Financial Analysts Journal.* He earned an undergraduate degree from Swarthmore College and an M.B.A. from Harvard University.

James R. Jundt, CFA, is director, chairman of the board, and CEO of Jundt Associates, an investment advisor. Previously, he acted as chairman of the board, president, and CEO of The Jundt Growth Fund, a closed-end fund that trades on the New York Stock Exchange. Mr. Jundt is a trustee of Gonzaga University.

Edward C. Mitchell, Jr., CFA, a partner and president of INVESCO Capital Management, is an original founder of INVESCO, which is now a global investment management firm. He began his career first as a security analyst and then as a portfolio manager with Citizens and Southern Investment Counseling, a wholly-owned subsidiary of Citizens and Southern Bank of Atlanta (now NationsBank). Mr. Mitchell earned a B.A. from the University of Virginia and an M.B.A. from the University of Colorado.

John B. Neff, CFA, is managing partner, senior vice president, executive committee member, and mutual fund portfolio manager of Wellington Management Company. He also serves as chairman of the investment board, a member of the executive committee, and a trustee of the University of Pennsylvania, and as a board of directors member of both General Accident F&L Assurance and the Global Utility Fund. Mr. Neff holds a B.B.A. from the University of Toledo, an M.B.A. from Case Western Reserve University, and an honorary M.A. from the University of Pennsylvania.

Patrick O'Donnell, Jr., is managing director and director of Equity Research at Putnam Investments. Before joining Putnam, Dr. O'Donnell was employed as a principal with Exeter Research, as both managing director of International Equities Research and a member of the board of directors at Prudential Securities, and as a vice president/analyst at Furman Selz, Donaldson, Lufkin & Jenrette, and E.F. Hutton. He earned a B.A. from Harvard College and a Ph.D. in English literature from Princeton University.

Claude N. Rosenberg, Jr., founded Rosenberg Capital Management (RCM), which primarily manages fixed-income and equity assets. RCM also formed the RREEF Corporation, which purchases high-quality, income-producing real estate for tax-exempt clients. Previously, Mr. Rosenberg was employed with J. Barth & Co., where he developed the largest investment research department in the western United

States. He is the author of several books, including *Stock Market Primer* and *The Common Way to Stock Market Profits*, as well as numerous articles on finance. Mr. Rosenberg is a former chairman of the advisory council of Stanford University and the recipient of Stanford's Ernest Arbuckle Award for Management Excellence. He received his B.A. and M.B.A from Stanford University.

Lewis A. Sanders, CFA, chairman and CEO of Sanford C. Bernstein & Company, has senior responsibility for research and investment management. He joined the company as a research analyst and has also served as research director, executive vice president, and president. Before his employment with Sanford C. Bernstein, Mr. Sanders served for two years as a research and administrative assistant at Oppenheimer & Co. Mr. Sanders earned a B.S. in operations research from Columbia University.

Warren E. Shaw, CFA, CEO and chief financial officer of Chancellor Capital Management, also acts as chairman of the Investment Policy Committee, which determines the firm's asset allocation strategy. Before assuming the position of CEO in 1995, he served Chancellor from 1973 to 1994 in various capacities, including as head of the Research Department's Capital Goods Unit, director of the Research Department, and head of the Equity Group. Mr. Shaw is a graduate of the Massachusetts Institute of Technology and holds an M.B.A. from Columbia University.

Jan R. Squires, CFA, is professor of finance and general business at Southwest Missouri State University. He has served AIMR in numerous capacities, recently acting as editor of the 1995 proceedings *Performance Evaluation, Benchmarks, and Attribution Analysis*. Dr. Squires has consulted with a variety of businesses and agencies and is the author and co-author of articles published in several journals, including the *Journal of Economics and Finance, Quarterly Journal of Economics and Business, Journal of Education for Business,* and *Bankers' Magazine*. He holds a B.S. and an M.A. from Central Missouri State University and a D.B.A. from the University of Virginia.

Value and Growth in Equity Investing: An Overview

Jan R. Squires, CFA
Professor of Finance
Southwest Missouri State University

Value and growth have been the two fundamental approaches to equity investing for more than half a century. These entrenched styles have evolved to the point at which they are used concurrently to describe entire money management strategies, portfolios and their contents, and even investment managers themselves. Yet, in some regards, value and growth are like many other widely used and accepted terms in various facets of life ("liberal" and "conservative" in the modern political landscape come to mind); "everybody knows" what the terms mean but almost no one stops occasionally to remember and affirm the terms' defining characteristics. Those who do stop to ask often find multiple definitions of the same term being used. "Everybody," it turns out, does not know what the terms mean; at least, they certainly do not ascribe the same meaning to the same term.

So, in the investment business, what do we truly mean when we use the terms "value" and "growth" to describe the way certain individuals and firms go about implementing strategies to serve the needs of clients? What are the defining characteristics, both conceptually and in practice, of the two styles? For example, do value investors look only at the levels of price multiples? How do or should value approaches reflect capitalization differences? Do growth investors focus on revenue or earnings growth? How does earnings momentum enter into the growth approach?

This proceedings is the product of an AIMR seminar designed to give participants a vehicle for considering these and many other questions about the two dominant investing styles. A major benefit of that consideration is that readers can reaffirm and reflect on the essential elements of each approach.

In the proceedings, some of the best known and most highly skilled proponents of the value and growth investing styles set forth their concepts of style and discuss the philosophies, strategies, and processes necessary to be successful in pursuing their styles. The speakers' willingness to share their hard-earned insights, to publicize what is in some cases the result of proprietary research, and to provide reasoned judgments about their approaches within the context of other investing approaches combine to create a unique opportunity to learn from some of the true "masters" of our profession.

Stanford Calderwood opens discussion of the value style by providing an overview of the various criteria used by index vendors to define value securities. Because nearly any definition of value can be used to outperform the S&P 500 Index, Calderwood concludes that superior information is a commodity. He evaluates empirical evidence showing that value has a positive bias versus growth—on average, about 300 basis points of outperformance and a larger bias for small-capitalization stocks. The value edge differs somewhat by size, index vendor, time horizon, and universe used, but it is enduring and is delivered with lower levels of risk than the returns associated with the growth style. The underlying reasons for value's positive bias, Calderwood concludes, are a yield premium, value analysts' reliance on hard data, the phenomenon of mean reversion, and most importantly, what he calls "mental demons," such as fear of regret.

William Fletcher continues the exploration of value investing with a look into the future of style investing in general. Although his firm is a traditional value-oriented firm, Fletcher is convinced that value versus growth may be an artificial distinction in the future in light of several emerging tensions in the industry and given inconclusive performance data for the two styles, at least when style index returns are examined. Clients increasingly see the return from any style index as a commodity and seek managers who can add value to that commodity return. Hence, Fletcher believes that managers should, as clients will, focus on skill-based investing, emphasizing a style-neutral, reproducible system for adding value to perhaps multiple benchmarks. He illustrates an approach to quantifying manager skill that focuses on the skills needed to produce certain performance results, and he shows how quantifying manager skill can be incorporated into attribution analysis.

Edward Mitchell shares with readers the basic beliefs and investment process followed by his value-oriented investment firm. INVESCO Capital Management's investment approach is grounded in the beliefs that markets are very efficient, that forecasting is fraught with difficulties, that stock prices are more volatile than the performance of the underlying companies, and that discipline is the key to any successful investing approach. Mitchell outlines the firm's valuation approach, which is based on the dividend discount model and incorporates an explicit risk-adjustment concept; he then uses examples from the pharmaceutical and utility sectors to illustrate the valuation approach. Mitchell also addresses stock selection and portfolio construction, including a discussion of the firm's rigorous sell discipline. Mitchell concludes with a list of "do's" and "don'ts" for the value manager.

In closing the value investing discussion, Lewis Sanders bases his value advocacy on three essential propositions: Value investing produces above-average returns, those results are enduring, and the benefits are obtainable globally. Certain widely displayed biases about wealth work to the advantage of value investors; namely, people overvalue certainty, overreact to big events with small probabilities of occurring, and are averse to loss. Sanders puts forth two axioms that drive the superior performance of value investing. First, value is a function of anxiety; empirical evidence on earnings revisions in the United States and other developed markets shows that the "domain of potential losses" (negative revisions) is where abnormal returns are earned. Second, mean reversion is strong; returns on equity in the United States and other markets revert strongly to the mean in relatively short periods of time. These factors help explain the value advantage, which Sanders documents by showing global premiums to value investing over time. Diversification benefits accrue as a bonus because the value premiums between markets are not highly correlated.

A link between the value and growth styles is provided by Patrick O'Donnell, who discusses the implications of the changing role of security analysts for the investment industry at large. Regardless of style, O'Donnell argues, many trends and pressures in the industry are causing the analyst role to evolve from an old model in which the analyst was in training for a "real" money management job to a new model in which security analysis is a professional career path with its own rewards and opportunities. This evolution has many implications for investment firm management, from the basic need to provide information resources and continuing education to analysts to such organizational changes as encouraging creativity and the willingness to admit mistakes, emphasizing forecasting, and fostering a culture in which conflict is productive. The latter is particularly important, O'Donnell asserts, because the changing analyst role involves several inherent conflicts, such as control versus creativity, habitual versus new understandings, group identity versus group think, and the need to know everything versus the need to know relevant information.

Parker Hall leads off the exploration of growth investing by noting that many investment firms with a growth investing focus have experienced remarkable increases in assets under management during the past 20 years. Evidence suggests that these firms did not sacrifice returns to achieve that asset growth; they matched or exceeded standard benchmark measures of performance. Hall elucidates seven organizational and operating characteristics common to the successful firms; three characteristics are fairly universal to all firms, and four draw specifically on the experiences of Hall's firm. Successful firms of whatever investing style or approach should reflect three defining characteristics: a clear statement of philosophy, fit with client objectives, and research to support the philosophy. The four remaining characteristics, although equally important, will reflect the uniqueness of each firm. First, firms must adhere to a clear decision-making process. Second, portfolio construction rules must be definitive and should reflect the firm's philosophy. Third, performance evaluation must be based on appropriate benchmarks considered over long time periods, and custom benchmarks may well be required. Fourth, motivation systems must emphasize long-term rewards for a long-term perspective.

James Jundt takes readers behind the scenes for a look at several of the unique characteristics of his growth-oriented firm. Although many valid approaches to the stock market exist, Jundt believes that the people and firms who have achieved good long-term results have some common ingredients in their approaches: They have philosophies they believe in; their operating structures are compatible with their philosophies and their personalities; and their implementation is consistent and disciplined on a long-term basis. Accordingly, the operating characteristics at Jundt Associates reflect the firm's mission. Jundt Associates carries out an intense search for companies with rapidly growing revenues, with geniuses at the helm, and with products and services responsive to societal changes. To pursue that search, the firm maintains a small and stable group of managers (all of whom are principals), follows a team approach, and assigns individuals to manage both small-cap and large-cap stocks. Jundt describes the current portfolio composition that reflects the firm's approach and discusses the firm's strictly enforced portfolio construction rules.

Claude Rosenberg argues that, in the past four decades or so, the business of growth stock investing has involved being at the right place at the right time and being patient in the face of unfavorable developments. The questions now are: Can growth stock investors rely on past practices in the future? And, where are the growth stocks of today and tomorrow? Rosenberg addresses these questions by first discussing basic principles of growth stock investing that appear to be timeless in nature. He then considers factors that may experience various changes over time. Among the timeless factors are low turnover, an emphasis on total returns, a focus on noncyclicals, and the importance of favorable macroeconomic conditions. Growth investors may need to rethink certain factors because of the increasing attractiveness of some cyclicals, a deemphasis on dividends, the importance of people rather than products, the critical nature of pricing power, and the importance of a corporate culture for growth. Rosenberg closes by identifying three characteristics of growth companies of the future and by summarizing analytical and behavioral lessons that will be important to the success of tomorrow's growth stock investors.

Warren Shaw wraps up the growth investing discussion by elaborating three major elements needed to execute a value-adding approach to growth stock investing in today's environment. First, successful execution reflects certain central convictions about investment philosophy and process—in Shaw's case, the importance of delivered growth, earnings momentum, and valuation. Second, the veritable blizzard of information available today must be organized in a way that will add value in terms of portfolio returns; Shaw distinguishes between forecast-based and fact-based research and also addresses the role of portfolio managers and investment committees in the information process. Third, research findings suggest that investors in growth companies should focus on what is truly important and truly adds value. Shaw presents empirical evidence to distinguish between high-expectation and low-expectation stocks (rather than growth versus value) and to illustrate the importance of earnings momentum—in and of itself and as a signal of delivered growth—in driving superior returns. He emphasizes the particular power of earnings momentum in the small-cap and medium-cap arenas and illustrates the importance of earnings momentum in the health care, retail, food/beverage/tobacco, and information processing sectors.

Although value and growth have often been portrayed as adversarial or mutually exclusive approaches, one of the benefits of this proceedings is that it highlights the common ground shared by these styles. Commitment to philosophy, reliance on rigorous research, a "big picture" perspective, constant innovation and improvement—these characteristics are traits that are truly independent of investing style and thus indicative of any successful style. Most importantly, the ideas set forth in this proceedings, and the enthusiasm of their contributors, reaffirm what is the most important shared characteristic of all—a single-minded focus on the client's financial well-being.

The Positive Bias for Value Investors in U.S. Equities

Stanford Calderwood
Chairman and CEO
Trinity Investment Management Corporation

Whatever the varied criteria used to define value, the historical record for performance gives an edge to value investing over growth investing. Empirical evidence demonstrates that value has a positive bias versus growth; factors that can help explain that positive bias include a yield premium, mean reversion, and behavioral principles such as fear of regret.

The historical performance of value investing versus growth investing decidedly favors the value style; both styles, however, are widely used and continue to enjoy ardent support, so value proponents apparently have not yet totally carried the day. This presentation provides an overview of the different value criteria used by value index vendors, evaluates the empirical evidence that value has a positive bias versus growth, and explores the underlying reasons for value's positive bias.

Value Benchmarks

The industry has no standard definitions for either value or growth investing; as shown in **Table 1**, however, the major vendors of style benchmarks and peer-group benchmarks use value criteria that are generally similar. Nevertheless, a vendor may use different criteria for establishing value in large-capitalization/value stocks and in small-capitalization/value stocks. Moreover, even when two vendors use essentially the same criteria, one vendor may classify a stock as growth and the other as value because of slight differences in construction methodologies.

The two benchmarks most commonly accepted by the business press are the S&P–BARRA Value Index—seen each week in *Forbes*—and the Russell 1000 Value Index—which appears in *Barron's*. Both are based on the work of William F. Sharpe and use price-to-book-value ratios (P/Bs) to designate value versus growth stocks. In general, both indexes rank a universe of stocks by their P/Bs and then classify stocks that are below the midpoint as value and those

above it as growth. At that point, however, the minor differences in methodologies begin to show up.

Frank Russell Company uses its 1000 Index as the basic universe; BARRA uses the S&P 500 Index. Therefore, a stock that is above the cutoff in the S&P 500, and thus classified as growth by BARRA, might well be below the cutoff in the 1000 Index and thus be classified as value by Russell.

In addition, when Russell introduced value and growth indexes for small-cap stocks within the Russell 2000, the methodology used for the large-cap stocks in the 1000 Index was inadequate. So many issues in the 2000 Index had no book value or negative book value that the Sharpe criterion did not work. Russell decided to use forecasted growth as well as P/B and give proportional classification to 1,000 of the 2,000 stocks.

Wilshire Associates introduced equity style portfolios in 1986 using the top 2,500 companies in the Wilshire 5000 universe and fundamental screens—P/E, P/B, and yield—to identify value stocks. At Wilshire, stocks that fell in the middle ground were simply eliminated.

Using any of these criteria, identifying stocks that will outperform the S&P 500 is so easy that managers at Trinity Investment Management feel comfortable saying, "Superior information is a commodity." For example, we conducted research covering 14 years—essentially, three complete peak-to-peak market cycles—using a simple 30 percent screen for the basic "value" criteria to discover their information content. At the start of each quarter, we created a portfolio consisting of the 30 percent of the S&P 500 stocks with the lowest P/Es (150

Table 1. Index Providers' Value Criteria

Index	Basic Criteria
S&P–BARRA Value	Low P/B
Russell 1000 Value	Low P/B
Russell 2000 Value	Low P/B
	Forecasted growth
	Proportional classification for 50% of list
Wilshire Large-Cap Value	Low P/B
	Low P/E
	High yield
	40% plus of top 750 *not* classified

Source: Trinity Investment Management Corp.

stocks in total). This buy list returned 17.5 percent on an annualized basis, outperforming the S&P 500's 13.3 percent by 4.2 percentage points. Some of that advantage stemmed from equal weighting of the buy list, but even measured against an equal-weighted S&P 500, the edge was still 1.7 points.

We went through exactly the same exercise using the bottom 30 percent of stocks ranked by P/B and then the top 30 percent of stocks ranked by yield. As **Figure 1** shows, all three of these buy lists outperformed the S&P 500—even when the equal-weighting advantage was removed.

Figure 1 also shows that when we combined all three approaches into a single composite, composed of about 50 issues that could meet all three value criteria, the value added was 6.8 percentage points. After tempering the results to take into account the impact of equal weighting and after allowing for implementation costs, the residual advantage had to be only about a single percentage point to put any of these buy lists in INDATA's top quartile for equity

managers,[1] hence the contention that superior information is a commodity.

The question is: If such superior information is so readily available, why is it not used more? And the answer is straightforward: Value investing based on these simple approaches contains many hidden aspects with which most managers have difficulty living. For example:

- A low-P/E strategy can create unacceptable volatility. For the year ending September 30, 1990, that particular buy list underperformed the S&P 500 by 17.5 percentage points.
- The low-P/B strategy has long negative horizons. That buy list, despite outperforming the S&P 500 by 4.8 percentage points annualized for the 14-year horizon, produced below-market returns for 4 consecutive calendar years.
- Using a composite of the three screens creates buy lists that have little diversification. In addition to averaging only 50 names, the composite had a 50 percent weight in just two sectors—utilities and finance.

In short, a lot of intestinal fortitude and patience are needed to stick with any of these screens.

Value versus Growth: The Empirical Evidence

Trinity has researched 13 matching pairs of value

[1]INDATA is a service of Gordon Haskett & Co., which analyzes institutional portfolios. The INDATA median manager return shown in Figure 1 thus applies to institutional equity portfolios. For the decade covered in Figure 1, beating the S&P 500 by only 0.8 percentage points yearly put a manager in INDATA's top quartile.

Figure 1. Four Outperforming Buy Lists Based on Simple Screens

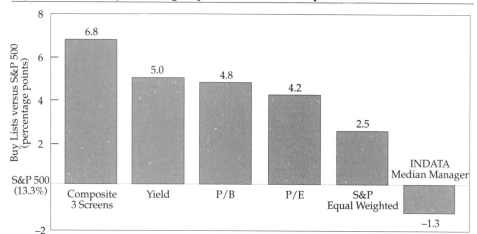

Note: Annualized data for 14 years ended 1994.

Source: Trinity Investment Management Corp.

and growth subindexes available in the U.S. equity market; these alternatives are subindexes, not peer-group benchmarks, and consist of 7 pairs for large-cap stocks and 3 pairs each for mid-cap and small-cap stocks. The average horizon for the 13 pairs was 21.1 years, ranging from 11 to 26 years, and the average return for the universes from which the pairs were drawn was 12.3 percent. The value side of each matching pair returned 14.1 percent as a group, and the growth side as a group returned 11.1 percent; in other words, the value side outperformed the universe by 180 basis points (bps) and the growth side by 300 bps, while the growth side underperformed the universe by 120 bps and the value side by 300 bps. These summary figures mask important size differences, however; value's biggest advantage comes in the small-cap arena, where the positive bias is 500 bps yearly, followed by mid-cap, where the bias is 290 bps, and large-cap, with a 220-bp advantage.

Returns by Size and Style

Table 2 shows, one-by-one, the 13 pairs of growth and value benchmarks ranked by large, medium, and small capitalization. The "VGS Research" entries in Table 2 are data from Trinity Investment Management's value/growth/size (VGS) study, first published in 1993 and updated quarterly. Trinity's VGS data come from a methodology similar to those of the other vendors; the study was undertaken primarily to make long horizons available. For horizons in which the VGS data overlap data from other indexes, the correlation of performance figures is high.

The key figures are in the last column of Table 2. Note that for *each* of the 13 matching pairs of value and growth benchmarks, value outperformed

growth. The difference in added value ranged from +0.5 to +6.9 percentage points. For all 13 matching pairs, the value style component outperformed the underlying universe during the period covered. For each vendor with matching pairs covering all three size categories, the positive spread between value and growth grew larger as the size dropped from the large-cap to the mid-cap and then to the small-cap categories. Twelve of the thirteen value benchmarks outperformed the S&P 500. The Russell 2000 value benchmark, while lagging the S&P by 2.6 percentage points, did outperform its underlying universe.

Variations in the Positive Style Bias

The positive bias of the value style does vary; the vendor's methodology, the horizon of the particular study, and the universe play a role. **Figure 2** focuses on the three matching pairs of style indexes available for mid-cap stocks. The raw data show value's advantage over growth to be 3.7 percentage points annualized in the VGS study but only 1.7 points in the Wilshire matching pairs. Several factors produce the differences.

First, none of the vendors' horizons match; they range from 17 years for the Wilshire data to 26 years for the VGS data. Second, agreement in defining a mid-cap universe is obviously lacking. Wilshire has 750 stocks in its mid-cap universe; BARRA has 1,430 stocks. The VGS uses the next 800 largest stocks below its large-cap stock category. This approach is similar to Russell's, but Russell does not as yet isolate value and growth in its mid-cap universe. Finally, as a result of these different horizons, the underlying universes all had varying base-line returns—ranging from 10.5 percent for the VGS data to 16.0 percent for

Table 2. Details of Value Return Bias

Source	Horizon Ending 12/30/94 (years)	Annualized Total Return					
		Universe	S&P 500	Value Stocks	Growth Stocks	Value versus Growth (percentage points)
VGS Research S&P 500	26.0	9.9%	10.1%	11.4%	9.2%	+2.2
VGS Research 1000	26.0	9.8	10.1	11.4	8.7	+2.7
VGS Research Large-Cap	26.0	9.3	10.1	10.4	8.8	+1.6
VGS Research Pure[a]	26.0	9.8	10.1	12.2	8.2	+4.0
S&P 500–BARRA	20.0	14.6	14.6	16.0	12.9	+3.1
Wilshire Large Company	17.0	14.1	14.2	15.1	14.6	+0.5
Russell 1000	16.0	14.6	14.7	15.1	14.0	+1.1
VGS Research Mid-Cap	26.0	10.5	10.1	12.1	8.4	+3.7
Sharpe/BARRA Medium	20.0	15.9	14.6	17.4	14.1	+3.3
Wilshire MidCap	17.0	16.0	14.2	17.8	16.1	+1.7
VGS Research Small-Cap	26.0	10.0	10.1	13.3	6.4	+6.9
Wilshire Small Company	17.0	16.0	14.2	19.5	15.7	+3.8
Russell 2000	11.0	9.7	13.6	11.8	7.4	+4.4
Average	21.1	12.3%	12.4%	14.1%	11.1%	+3.0

[a]Without the 20 percent of issues that are in the buffer zone—that is, stocks that have a percentage of total share classified as value and growth.

Source: Trinity Investment Management Corp.

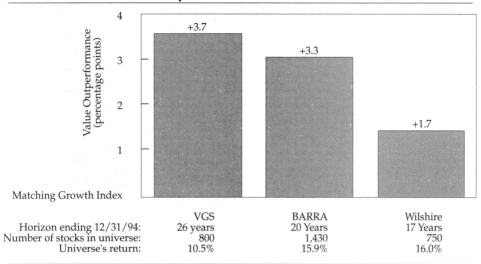

Figure 2. Value's Positive Bias by Methodology, Horizon, and Universe: Mid-Cap Value versus Mid-Cap Growth Indexes

	VGS	BARRA	Wilshire
Horizon ending 12/31/94:	26 years	20 Years	17 Years
Number of stocks in universe:	800	1,430	750
Universe's return:	10.5%	15.9%	16.0%

Source: Trinity Investment Management Corp.

Wilshire's mid-cap universe.

In light of these differences, the need for both the manager and the sponsor to agree on the indexable alternative to be used as a benchmark is critical. Recognizing the effects of different horizons would be a key part of assessing potential indexes; accordingly, we analyzed nine matching pairs of value and growth indexes for the common 16-year horizon ending in 1994. The Russell small-cap indexes were eliminated because their histories go back only 11 years, and the VGS pure value category was not used because its annual reconstitution and resulting turnover preclude it from being a truly viable indexing alternative. The Wilshire pairs likewise cannot be considered truly "indexable," but we included them simply because what Wilshire calls style portfolios carry essentially index fund fees and many clients consider them essentially index funds. **Table 3** shows that for 11 of the 16 years, value's positive bias increases as the size category goes down. In this horizon, the spread between large-cap/value and large-cap/growth is 1.4 percentage points, whereas the spread between small-cap/value and small-cap/growth is 5.9 points.

Risk and Styles

In addition to total performance, we looked at the risk characteristics of value and growth investing. All comparisons were annualized for the 13 growth/value benchmark pairs and made relative to the S&P 500 for the available horizons of each benchmark.

As **Table 4** shows, not only does the value style have a built-in positive bias in terms of absolute performance for the relevant period measured, but

that outperformance comes with considerably less risk than the growth style. The value indexes as a group delivered their 300 bps superior performance with roughly 20 percent less standard deviation and more than 20 percent smaller betas. The winning percentage of trailing three-year horizons (defined as the percentage of positive performance versus the S&P 500 for trailing-year horizons ending December 30, 1994) for value is almost twice that of growth. The average shortfall for value from the S&P 500 for trailing three-year horizons is only 3.2 percentage points, 30 percent less than growth.

Summary of Research Findings

The 13-pair comparison of value and growth benchmarks just discussed is not the only research to show a positive bias for the value style. The findings

Table 3. Value's Annual Return Bias, 1979–94

Index	Value Index	Growth Index	Value versus Growth (percentage points)
Large-cap average	15.4%	14.0%	+1.4
VGS 1000	15.4	13.1	+2.3
S&P–BARRA	15.2	13.9	+1.3
Russell 1000	15.1	14.0	+1.1
Wilshire	15.7	14.9	+0.8
Mid-cap average	16.8	14.7	+2.1
Wilshire	18.3	15.8	+2.5
VGS	16.6	14.2	+2.4
Sharpe/BARRA	15.5	14.1	+1.4
Small-cap average	19.0	13.1	+5.9
VGS	17.9	11.2	+6.7
Wilshire	20.0	15.0	+5.0

Source: Trinity Investment Management Corp.

Table 4. Risk and Return Comparison: Benchmark Pairs versus S&P 500

13 Benchmarks	Averages		Comments
	Growth	Value	
Returns versus S&P (percentage points)	−1.3	1.7	Value: +3.0
Risk measures			
Standard deviation	20.7	16.6	Value 20% less
Beta	1.23	0.95	Value 23% less
Standard error	7.1	6.9	Similar volatility
Winning percentage			
Trailing one year	39.8	58.6	Value 47% ahead
Trailing three years	31.5	61.2	Value even better
Average shortfall			
Trailing one year	−6.2	−6.3	Similar
Trailing three years	−4.4	−3.2	Value 27% better

Source: Trinity Investment Management Corp.

of four other studies, written in the late 1960s and 1970s, are summarized in **Table 5**. In the study with the longest horizon (33 years), Graham defined value as the lowest third of the DJIA ranked by P/Es and defined growth as the top third. Nicholson defined value as the lowest P/E quintiles and growth as the top quintiles. Miller and Basu also used P/E quintiles to define value and growth. The annual spread returns found in these studies are consistent with the findings reported here.

Trinity's 26-year VGS style study combined with the four studies shown in Table 5 represent 58 years of data, from 1937 through 1994. Although every analysis is subject to a horizon bias, we believe this research shows a uniform and strong case for value investing: On average, for 13 pairs of matching indexes, with an average horizon for the studies of 21.1 years, value outperformed growth by 300 bps annualized. Other findings are (1) value's positive bias versus growth varies with the source and universe used; (2) the differential increases for mid-cap and small-cap stocks; and (3) value is less risky than growth—by about 20 percent based on beta and standard deviation—and wins more often with no

more pronounced shortfall.

The Underlying Reasons for Value's Bias

Many reasons explain value's positive bias. This section divides them into four categories, but the reasons are interrelated. Perhaps the most important reason—but the hardest to pinpoint—is the element of human behavior in the decision-making process.

Value's Yield Premium

Results based on the Ibbotson Associates data base for the 69 years ending December 30, 1994, shown in Panel A of **Table 6**, indicate that roughly half the total return on common stocks is attributable to the yield component. The market's yield of 4.9 percent annualized over the past 69 years accounted for about 48 percent of the index's total return. Only a 5.3 percent return was needed from capital appreciation to deliver the index's total return of 10.2 percent.

Ibbotson does not classify stocks by growth and value, but data for the Russell Value and Growth indexes for the trailing 14 years ending 1994 show

Table 5. Evidence for the Value Bias for Horizons before 1972

Value–Growth Annual Return Spread	Horizon	Study
9.4%	33 years (1937–69)	Benjamin Graham, low- versus high-P/E thirds within DJIA, *Intelligent Investor*, 1973.
13.0	26 years (1937–62)	Francis Nicholson, low- versus high-P/E quintiles, *Financial Analysts Journal, The Journal of Finance*, 1968.
10.7	17 years (1948–64)	Paul Miller, low- versus high-P/E quintiles, Drexel & Co., 1966.
7.0	15 years (1957–71)	Sanjoy Basu, low- versus high-P/E quintiles, *The Journal of Finance*, June 1977.

Source: Trinity Investment Management Corp.

Table 6. Value and Growth Yields

A. Ibbotson data

Return	Contribution	Percent Share
Yield/reinvested yield	4.86%	47.7%
Capital appreciation	5.33	52.3
Total return	10.19%	100.0%

B. Pro forma yields

Component	Share Contribution in S&P 500	Adjusted by Style Growth	Adjusted by Style Value
Yield	47.7%	32.3%	61.9%
Capital appreciation	52.3	67.7	38.1

Sources: Trinity Investment Management Corp.; *Stocks, Bonds, Bills, and Inflation* (Chicago, Ill.: Ibbotson Associates, 1995).

Table 7. Yield's Role in Total Return: 14 Years Ended December 30, 1994

Characteristic	Lowest Yield	Highest Yield
S&P 500 equal-weighted total returns	14.9%	14.9%
Test portfolios' equal-weighted total returns	9.2	17.9
Portfolios versus equal-weighted S&P 500	−5.7	+3.0
Standard deviation	23.2	15.0
Average yield	0.39	6.80
Average P/E	16.22×	10.01×
Average P/B	1.47×	1.11×
Average long-term growth	15.7	8.7
Average market cap ($billions)	$2.3	$5.4
Average beta	1.33×	0.85×
Quarters ahead of S&P 500	26	35
Percent of total 56 quarters	46.4%	62.5%

Source: Trinity Investment Management Corp.

that, on average, the yield premium for value stocks has been 29.6 percent whereas the yield discount for growth stocks has averaged 32.3 percent. Using those data to adjust the last column of the Ibbotson data produces Panel B of Table 6. Simply to match the market, the growth manager must squeeze 67.7 percent of the target out of the capital appreciation component, by far the harder result to achieve. From time to time, dividends are cut, but on balance, dividends grow and are much easier to identify and lock in than is capital appreciation. In contrast, the value manager need get only 38.1 percent of the target out of the appreciation component. In essence, the value manager can lock in 61.9 percent of the target because of the average 29.6 percent yield premium enjoyed by value stocks.

Another way of understanding the role yield plays in value investing is to isolate high yield from all other fundamentals associated with value stocks. (Managers do not generally use high yield as the only criterion, but that "above-market yield" is a key variable.) Focusing on the role of yield for the 14 years ending December 30, 1994, and using the S&P 500 as our universe, we created two equal-weighted portfolios. One is based on the 20 percent of the S&P 500 stocks with the highest yield within each sector at the start of each quarter, and the other is based on the 20 percent of the S&P stocks with the lowest yield within each sector at the start of each quarter. The performance and risk characteristics of these high- and low-yield lists are compared in **Table 7**. The highest yield stocks outperformed the S&P 500 by 300 bps and more than 60 percent of the time while the lowest yield stocks underperformed the universe by 570 bps and nearly half the time; the high-yield stocks' average beta was roughly 40 percent lower than that of the low-yield group, and the standard deviation was lower by approximately one-third.

High yield is, of course, only one piece of the mosaic that constitutes what is generally accepted as a value stock. A stock could easily have a high yield for reasons other than undervaluation. The company

could be in serious financial trouble, the price could be down, or the dividend might not have been cut as it should. Also, Table 7 reflects other factors at work. Because the 20 percent of the stocks with the lowest yield have a market capitalization that is nearly 60 percent below that of the higher yielding stocks, the low-yield list will be affected by the small-cap effect. For this particular horizon, small-cap stocks lagged the S&P 500 by about 1.9 percentage points yearly. Even with these caveats, however, Table 7 underscores the important role high yield plays in value investing's positive bias.

The Benefit of Hard Data

Another reason for the positive bias of the value style may stem from value managers' use of existing, known data rather than estimates. Value managers place little dependence on what the future holds. In contrast, the information growth managers use is based primarily on forecasts—and history shows that those forecasts are not very reliable.

The vendors of style benchmarks agree that three major characteristics differentiate value and growth styles. First, the value investment approach focuses on known fundamentals and seeks to identify, not future rewards, but present value: below-market P/Bs and P/Es and above-market dividend yields. The driving determinants for value stocks are solid data with a history of being reasonably accurate. The investors can depend on the data being used to be reasonably reliable and consistent across all companies because of Financial Accounting Standards Board rules or SEC filing requirements.

Growth investors focus on favorable expectations—expected high short-term and long-term growth in earnings per share (EPS)—and they are dependent on forecasting market and general economic scenarios. Whereas virtually all analysts and researchers would agree on a P/B for a particular stock, forecasted earnings can, and do, vary widely. The academic literature is replete with studies showing the inaccuracy of earnings estimates. A ballpark figure is that average estimates are off plus or minus about 30 cents for every dollar of actual earnings. Trinity recently studied the accuracy and optimism/pessimism of consensus one-year earnings estimates for 334 large-cap stocks for a ten-year period ending in 1993. We found a mean absolute error of 25 percent, with about 65 percent above-actual estimates and about 34 percent below-actual estimates. In addition to the difficulties in forecasting earnings, given the necessary two-stage forecasting of growth investing—first forecasting a scenario and then forecasting which stocks will do well in such a scenario—the variations seem almost infinite.

Regression to the Mean

The statistical phenomenon of regression to the mean was first observed more than 100 years ago by Sir Francis Galton, a pioneer in eugenics. Since Galton's time, regression to the mean has been documented in areas ranging from the batting averages of ball players to the prices of stocks. Although the return on common stocks can swing widely up and down, in the long haul, the return will be roughly the 10 percent mean shown in long-term studies such as the Cowles Commission study and Ibbotson Associates research.

The role of regression to the mean in value investing's positive bias was shown in a study we conducted comparing the historical averages of three key fundamentals—P/B, P/E, and yield—for the Russell 1000 Value and Growth indexes with the S&P 500 mean values for those fundamental factors. The study, reported in **Figure 3**, covered the 14-year period ending December 31, 1994. The first findings were that the P/B for growth stocks was nearly 68 percent greater than the market's P/B and the P/B for value stocks was more than 25 percent smaller; that is, there is about 2.5 times more regression pressure on growth stocks than on value stocks. By definition, as this fundamental for growth regresses to the mean, stock price drops; for value stocks, regression of P/B to the mean implies a price increase.

The same relationships, regression pressures, and conclusions hold for P/E and yield. For all three fundamental factors, regression to the market mean implies a price increase for value stocks and a price decline for growth stocks.

Regression to the mean can come quickly and be very severe, especially for high-flying growth stocks. The $25.1 billion drop in market capitalization for Merck & Company over a trailing year ended July 30, 1993, illustrates:

	7/31/92	7/30/93
Quality rating	A+	A+
Share price	$51.87	$30.62
EPS estimate for next 12 months	$2.35	$2.55
P/B	10.7×	6.7×
P/B versus S&P 500	+346.0%	+100.0%
Price/EPS	22.1×	12.0×
Price/EPS versus S&P 500	+100.0%	−35.0%
Market capitalization ($billions)	$60.0	$34.9

Figure 3. Regression to the Market Mean: 1980–94 Premium/Discount of Russell 1000 Index versus S&P 500 Index

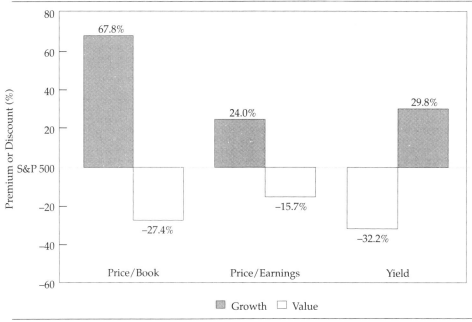

Source: Trinity Investment Management Corp.

In July 1992, Merck's P/B was 346 percent higher than the S&P 500's and far above the average premium of 68.3 percent for growth stocks in general. Merck's price peaked in July 1992 when the estimate for the next 12 months was $2.35, for a P/E multiple of 22.1. Merck's slide started in mid-August 1992 when all drug stocks were under price pressure in anticipation of health care changes expected from the Clinton administration, and the slide continued during the next 12 months. With analysts expressing concern about an unexpected slow start for a new drug, Merck's total return lagged the market by nearly 50 percent.

One wonders whether the stock price would have fallen so far so quickly had the P/Bs and P/Es not been at such lofty levels in the beginning. In any case, Merck is but one of many examples of how growth stocks can take very big hits on very modest news.

"Mental Demons"

Some psychologists, notably Daniel Kahneman and Amos Tversky, have been researching human behavior in the decision-making process for years, but only in the last decade or so have academics started linking that research to the investment process. Although Kahneman and Tversky did not focus on investors in particular, many of their insights apply to the decisions investors are constantly required to make, and finance scholars have increasingly drawn on those insights in recent years. For example, in *Advances in Behavioral Finance*, roughly half of the 21 reprinted papers draw on work by Kahneman and Tversky.[2]

The title of this subsection comes from a review appearing in *Fortune* of several psychological studies related to investing; the authors of the review concluded that irrational behavior can cause bad buy-and-sell decisions and called the phenomenon "mental demons at work."[3] Irrational behavior can be harmful to both growth and value stocks, and no research has attempted to distinguish whether the negative impact is greater for one investment style or another. We believe, however, that irrationality takes a bigger toll in growth investing than in value investing.

We considered three primary demons in the context of active growth and value managers:

- Investors prize certainty, glamour, and the comfort of the consensus.
- Fear of losses exceeds investors' aversions to risk.

- Remote possibilities tend to be exaggerated and stimulate overreaction.

■ *The comfort of the consensus.* A primary manifestation of the comfort of the consensus is an emotional factor termed by Meir Statman and others the "fear of regret." It may contribute to the popularity of glamorous stocks, and it often has a paralyzing effect. The factor works as follows: If an investor buys a depressed stock—a steel company today or an oil service company—and the stock price declines farther, the investor thinks, "How could I have been so dumb?" But if the investor buys an admired stock—say, IBM—and it declines, the investor considers the drop an act of God and thinks, "It's not my fault." The result is that sometimes investors and managers seek the comfort of the consensus and purchase mediocre big-name stocks; that is, they "park" some of the portfolio's assets in popular stocks. At the same time, they often avoid issues that are poorly regarded.

This tendency could have different effects on value and growth stocks because growth managers tend to favor the highly regarded issues with the good stories while value managers search for the undiscovered—maybe discarded—values.

IBM is a good example of this power of the consensus. In 1970, IBM had the largest market capitalization of any U.S. company and was the largest single holding in most institutional portfolios. IBM's earnings and growth appeared strong. Ten years later, the stock had underperformed the S&P 500 by 59.6 percentage points, or 3.3 points annualized. Despite this poor performance, managers remained leery of going without the giant, and IBM still ranked as the largest stock by market capitalization.

IBM's performance during the next decade was twice as bad as the previous decade; it underperformed the S&P 500 by 119.9 percentage points, or 4.4 points annualized. But IBM remained the largest stock.

After another large shortfall in 1991 (48.1 percentage points), IBM finally fell from the top spot—but only to 8th place. After continued poor performance (a shortfall of 47.6 percentage points) in 1992, it finally fell to 14th. Finally, the fear of regret had faded as a motivating force, but only in the face of sustained, almost shocking, underperformance.

Other examples of investors prizing certainty, glamour, and the comfort of the consensus come from Barry Bannister's follow-up study of the 62 companies cited in *In Search of Excellence: Lessons from America's Best Run Companies*.[4] Bannister used Peters

[2]See Richard H. Thaler, ed., *Advances in Behavioral Finance* (New York: Russell Sage Foundation, 1993).

[3]John J. Curran, "Why Investors Make the Wrong Choices," *Fortune Investors Guide* (1987).

[4]See Thomas J. Peters and Robert H. Waterman (New York: Harper & Row, 1982); and Barry B. Bannister, "In Search of Excellence: A Portfolio Management Perspective," *Financial Analysts Journal* (March/April 1990).

and Waterman's definition of excellence to study the investment value of the "excellent companies." He focused on six financial measures to rate each company: compound asset growth; compound equity growth; average returns on sales, total capital, and equity; and average ratio of market value to book value. Bannister reconstructed the S&P 500 for each year from 1977 through 1989 as it appeared at year-end and calculated the six variables for each company. The companies ranked in the top third in all six categories were put into an equally weighted portfolio for each year. Bannister also created portfolios of the "unexcellent" companies, defined as those that ranked in the bottom third in all six categories.

The three-year relative returns of the excellent portfolios versus the S&P 500 for various horizons were as follows:

6/77–6/80	27.0%
6/78–6/81	13.7
6/79–6/82	13.7
6/80–6/83	–10.0
6/81–6/84	–12.2
6/82–6/85	–29.8
6/83–6/86	–37.3
6/84–6/87	–21.8
6/85–6/88	–32.2
6/86–6/89	–15.2

The excellent companies outperformed in the first three horizons, possibly because of the high interest rates and inflation of that period, which would have taken a toll on weak companies. In the last seven horizons, however, the excellent companies underperformed the S&P 500. The excellent portfolios also underperformed the unexcellent portfolio, which outperformed the S&P 500 for the period by an average of 15 percentage points. The excellent portfolio trailed the unexcellent portfolio in eight of the ten periods.

Bannister concluded that previous financial strength will propel a stock into favor with glamour-based, growth investors, thereby making the stock expensive to buy. Better bargains exist in the out-of-favor value names. Intuition and common sense suggest that the comfort of the consensus, particularly the fear of regret, might well be playing a role in the value style's long-term positive bias.

■ *Fear of losses.* Kahneman and Tversky asked subjects to choose between different pairs of risks and rewards:

1. *Which alternative would you take?*
   A. a sure loss of $3,000 or
   B. an 80 percent chance of losing $4,000 and a 20 percent chance of losing nothing.

2. *Would you take this bet on a coin toss?*
   A. heads you win $1,500.

B. tails you lose $1,000.

For the first question, the expected return is determined by subtracting the $3,000 sure loss from the 80 percent chance of losing $4,000. If the second choice is taken consistently, the chooser will be behind by $3,200 – $3,000, or a total of $200. Most of the subjects made the second choice. Despite being riskier, the second choice offers a small chance of losing nothing.

For the second question, the potential payoff of $1,500 is 1.5 times the potential loss of $1,000. Nevertheless, most of Kahneman and Tversky's subjects refused to bet. How can otherwise rational people act so unwisely in the face of promising money-making opportunities? Kahneman and Tversky concluded that most people are put off by the 50 percent chance of losing. The researchers called this loss aversion "a surprisingly powerful emotion"; they considered it so great, in fact, that it keeps people from accepting good bets either in flipping coins or in selecting stocks.

Lewis Sanders argues that excessive loss aversion helps explain why certain stocks become deeply undervalued. He notes that investors can easily imagine that already depressed stocks with below-market P/Bs could decline still farther. Even when the stock prices drop to bargain-basement levels—a condition generally associated with the value style—investors steer clear.[5]

Therefore, we suspect that this behavioral factor could help account for the value style's positive bias. Such behavior might well make the value stock segment of the market less efficient than the growth segment, and managers who can handle the fear of loss could well be taking advantage of that inefficiency. The fear of losses on the part of some investors can lead to opportunities for profit for other investors; value managers look for a strong company with sound fundamentals, buy the stock after its price has been unduly depressed, and profit when the market realizes it has overreacted.

■ *Exaggeration of remote possibilities.* Fortune's review of Kahneman and Tversky's work noted that "while some mental demons can keep us from buying cheap stocks, others work the opposite way, nudging us into the wrong ones." Kahneman and Tversky asked subjects to choose one of two possibilities:

1. a 2 percent chance to win $3,000 or

2. a 1 percent chance to win $6,000.

The payoff for either choice is exactly the same, $60, but people do not see it that way. The second choice won by a 2-to-1 margin. The less likely the long-term payoff, Kahneman and Tversky concluded, the more

---

[5]See Mr. Sanders presentation, pp. 28–34.

mental calculations break down, causing overestimation of its probability.

In the stock market, this syndrome can lead investors to undervalue and to overvalue stocks. One example of the former is the case of Union Carbide. In 1984, a gas leak at Union Carbide's plant in Bhopal, India, killed thousands of people. Despite the strong financial condition of the company before the accident, investors predicted Union Carbide would be severely damaged by negative publicity, lawsuits, and penalties. That year, the stock underperformed the market by 43.8 percent as investors scrambled to unload the company's stock. By the end of the next year, however, the stock had regained its previous loss and outperformed the market by 75.2 percent. In the second year, the stock outperformed the S&P 500 by 43.4 points. Investors who saw the stock as undervalued and bought it after the accident obtained a big payoff.

Exaggeration of remote possibilities can also lead investors to overvalue stock. In the case of Genentech, for example, a company with a new heart drug yet to be approved by the U.S. Food and Drug Administration, investor enthusiasm drove the stock up about three times in less than a year. The stock at its peak had a P/E of 395 times! *Fortune* quoted one value style manager who would not buy the stock as saying, "Investors are not betting that the new drug will be successful. They are betting on the remote possibility that it will be a blockbuster and will not encounter competition." The return on Genentech stock was 71.9 percent greater than the S&P 500 in 1985 and 125.3 percent greater in 1986. Then, sure enough, harsh reality set in, and the stock dropped 85.1 percentage points versus the market during 1987 and 1988.

By definition, the overreaction factor is asymmetrical. Investors overreacting to good news about earnings or other specific company news can react with excessive optimism that can drive a stock up 100 percent, 200 percent, or even more, but overreaction to bad news has a floor: The price of a stock—value or growth—cannot go down more than 100 percent.

For value stocks, when future earnings turn out to be worse than expected, share prices are apt to fall less than would be the case for growth stocks with disappointing earnings. The reason is that unreasonably optimistic forecasts tend to generate bigger price increases for growth stocks than for value stocks. When the bad news hits, growth stocks have much farther to move down because the previous overreaction took the price so high.

Conclusion

For value managers, superior information is a commodity. The empirical evidence is overwhelming that value has a built-in positive bias versus growth, and that positive bias is based on logical realities not enjoyed by the growth style.

Exploiting value's positive bias, however, is not easy. Growth stocks can be tempting; fund sizes can force suboptimal style or size exposures; and large sector holdings can often strain diversification guidelines. The major challenge for investors and portfolio managers, of course, is getting value's positive bias into portfolios.

Value Investing in a Style-Neutral World

William C. Fletcher, CFA
President and Chief Investment Officer
Independence Investment Associates, Inc.

Despite the ongoing debate about the relative merits of value versus growth investing, the omens are that clients and the investment community will care less and less about styles in the future. Instead, the focus will be on skill-based investing and those managers who can demonstrate reproducible value-adding skills that transcend current style notions. The data discussed here indicate that, whatever style is being used, stock selection is the skill that adds value more consistently and more easily than the other investing disciplines.

In the next five to ten years, the investment community in general, and clients in particular, will not care as much about styles as they have in the past. Instead, the focus will be on *skill-based* investing, and clients will search out those managers whose demonstrated skills in adding value transcend current notions of investment "style." This presentation develops the expected changes by profiling a traditional value-oriented investing approach, then describing a contrasting skill-based investing approach and the skill-based value manager of the future.

The Value Approach at Independence Investment Associates

Value managers are frequently thought to be highly quantitative managers. Independence Investment managers are no exception. Underlying this trait, in our case, is a strong conviction about the kind of stocks we want to own: The stocks must be cheap, a criterion of all value managers, but not because the companies are falling apart. Thus, the investment process at Independence involves finding undervalued securities with improving fundamentals. This process integrates fundamental research (i.e., judgments about future fundamentals) and quantitative valuation techniques to develop a list of securities, ranked from best to worst, from which we create diversified portfolios. The highest ranked stocks on this list at any given time are cheap stocks that have had some measurable improvement in their underlying business fundamentals.

Important indicators of cheapness are high growth relative to observed P/E multiples, a rising dividend stream, a low current P/E (in historical context), and high asset values. These indicators are used in many traditional valuation models—discounted cash flow, relative P/E, and price to book value. Many conventional methods also exist to assess a company's fundamentals. Independence emphasizes signs of earnings momentum, such as accelerating earnings growth, positive earnings surprises, and favorable cyclical timing as reflected in economic factors. The secret is not in any one of the models but in their application and implementation: How good are a manager's inputs into the process, and how well does the manager use the information?

Although Independence is biased toward using quantitative techniques, the results of analysts' research are essential to understanding future trends. Without that understanding, one is condemned to repeating historical trends. Investment decisions at Independence thus reflect those forecasts—but in a very disciplined way and always within the context of focusing on *cheapness* and *improving fundamentals*.

Value versus Growth: The Wrong Question?

In the past decade, successfully running an investment management firm, including Independence, has required only three simple steps: assembling great talent, developing a philosophy that makes sense (and sticking to it), and serving clients well. This approach will not be sufficient in the next decade. Several elements are missing from the old formula.

First is the tension created in balancing the seemingly unique abilities of the individual "star" manager, to whom clients may well have been attracted in the first place, against the needs and demands of today's clients for a reproducible investment process—one that will go on despite individual personalities. Second is the tension that results when a single, very focused philosophy tends to lead, as it almost inevitably does, to a single product at a time when the market seemingly wants multiple products from the larger organizations. The third tension occurs in addressing the question of whether clients hire investment managers to manage money or to manage overall firm-to-firm relationships. Certainly, this list does not comprise all the relevant conflicts, and not all three may apply to all firms, but even casual conversations with clients will impart a sense of these trends to discerning managers.

What Do Clients Expect?

Proponents of either the growth or the value style approach can make a case for their superior performance. For example, **Figure 1** uses the Frank Russell indexes to show the performance difference between the value and growth approaches; in some years, value managers outperformed, and in other years, growth managers outperformed.

Figure 2 illustrates the same pattern in median manager performance. This figure uses data from Callan Associates to compare the return performance of median value and median growth managers; again, the evidence suggests that one style outperforms for a period and then the other style is superior.

More importantly, what do clients expect of value (or growth) managers? Clients can always buy a style index, so getting the return expected from the *style* is nothing more than a commodity. If 1995 turns out to be a great value (or growth) year, the client will not really care. From the client's perspective, that fact is largely irrelevant. Increasingly, the only thing clients care about is the *value added* above and beyond the benchmark. Clients have, in effect, taken away the natural advantage of value investing—the inherent advantage that comes from the approach most value managers follow, namely, the tilt toward low P/Es and high yields and/or book values.

What Do Clients Get?

In this context of client expectations for superior performance as measured against a benchmark rather than against another style, the question is: How have value managers and their clients fared? **Figure 3** plots the performance of the Callan median value manager against the benchmark, the Russell 1000 Value Index. The evidence is mixed; in many years, the median value manager did outperform the index, but in other years, the manager did not. The correlation coefficient for the two sets of returns is only about 0.63, so the value manager certainly did not track the value benchmark as well as clients might have hoped.

Figure 4, which reports the historical difference between manager and index returns, reveals the same inconsistent performance. When added value is measured by the difference between median value manager performance and value index performance, the median manager is found to have added value only about half the time during the 1979–94 period. To address specifically whether value managers add value in a good-value-investing environment, **Figure 5** focuses on the value added by the median value manager *in those years when value outperformed growth*. Since 1979, value managers have underperformed their benchmarks in almost every good-value-invest-

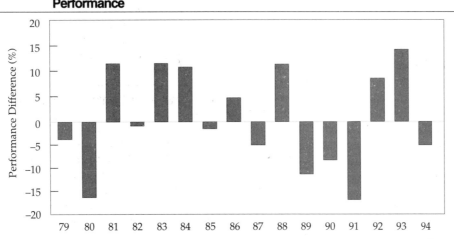

Figure 1. Russell 1000 Value Index versus Russell 1000 Growth Index: Historical Performance

Source: Independence Investment Associates, based on data from Frank Russell Company.

Figure 2. Median Value Manager versus Median Growth Manager: Historical Performance

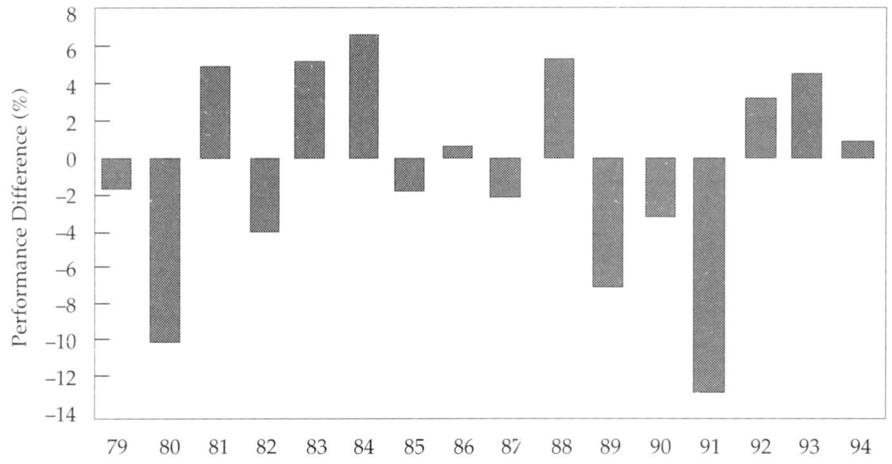

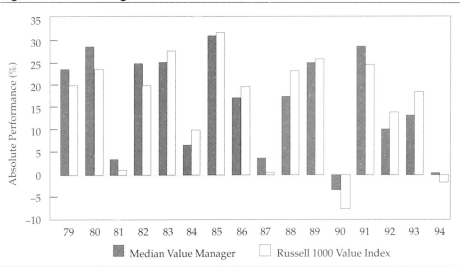

Source: Independence Investment Associates, based on data from Callan Associates.

Figure 3. Value Manager Performance versus Russell 1000 Value Index

Source: Independence Investment Associates.

ing year. That is, when it mattered most to clients, value managers as a group underperformed. How are clients likely to interpret these results?

No wonder clients complain that they cannot find a value manager that consistently outperforms the value index. Clients now view the return to the benchmark as a commodity; active managers must add value. Moreover, they must add it consistently. If clients cannot find a value manager with a reproducible process that gives them confidence in future returns, they will revert to the index.

Skill-Based Investing

In the past, clients covered their bases by selecting a variety of managers that each followed a particular style. They picked a good value manager and a good growth manager, a large-capitalization manager and a small-capitalization manager. In the future, however, clients will focus on a new type of manager—one that is not style specific but is skillful in adding value to several style benchmarks.

This emphasis on skill-based investing changes the rules of the game and raises a critical issue for managers themselves: How can value managers convince clients they have that kind of skill? For that matter, can any investment management firm provide individual managers who are skillful in all styles? Numerous firms offer multiple products or have divisions that offer particular styles, but can a firm work within a single philosophy that is not style specific? I believe that the investment management firm of the future will have that capability.

Figure 4. Value Added by Median Value Manager

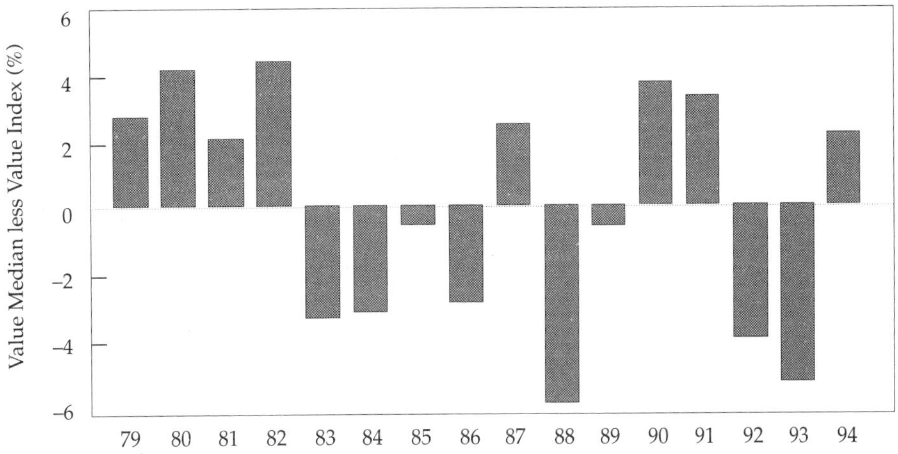

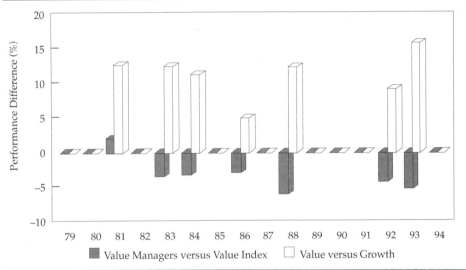

Source: Independence Investment Associates.

Figure 5. Value Added in Good Years

Source: Independence Investment Associates.

Style-Specific versus Style-Neutral Investment Philosophy

Skill-based investing requires differentiation between those investment philosophies that are inherently limiting, or style specific, and those that are generalizable, or style neutral. The style-specific philosophies are characterized by restriction to a single benchmark type for comparison purposes. The style-neutral philosophy is not; in fact, it may encourage multiple benchmarks.

For example, a manager may have a conviction that the way to superior performance is always to buy large-cap stocks with low P/Es, high book values, and high yields. This philosophy may work well at times, but this manager may be limited by that conviction. The manager may not be able to transfer the skills of large-cap/value investing to adding

value through growth management.

A style-neutral manager, in contrast, may follow the philosophy that superior performance is achieved by identifying cheap stocks that, regardless of their traditional "style" assignment, display increasing earnings momentum. Such a philosophy can be layered on top of any benchmark, allowing the manager to manage, for example, core, growth, value, and medium-cap portfolios. These portfolios can be measured against multiple indexes, and they focus on the client's mandate to separate value-added skill from the pure commodity return of a particular style.

Skills that are at center stage in a style-specific world—market timing, industry rotation, and individual expertise—will be de-emphasized in a style-neutral setting. Premiums will be paid to those with demonstrated skills in pure stock selection and in the design and delivery of reproducible (that is, attributable to skill), style-neutral implementation disciplines.

Quantifying Skill-Based Investing

These different skills, and the performance of skill-based managers in general, will also be subject to measurement by somewhat different methods than have been used in the style-specific context. Assessment of skill-based investing involves three simple concepts: the information coefficient, expected excess return (alpha), and the information ratio.

The *information coefficient* ("I.C.") is a measure of the manager's skill—a correlation of the manager's predictions of individual stock returns and the actual outcomes. The *alpha* (or realized excess return) is a function of the manager's skill level (or I.C.), of the volatility of the possible outcomes, and of breadth (or the number of decisions the manager is making). The *information ratio* compares alpha with the standard deviation of alpha, *ex post*; in other words, the information ratio provides an after-the-fact comparison of value added and volatility.

Figure 6 examines the potential breadth (number of decisions) and volatility of three investing approaches. In terms of breadth, a market timer makes one decision—to be in or out of the market—in any time frame. In terms of volatility, the decision will either be very right or very wrong; the decision will have a very large positive or negative impact—a volatile outcome. An industry rotator makes perhaps 16 industry or sector bets at any one time; the decisions have large impacts but not as extreme as the market-timing effects. A pure stock picker with a 100-stock portfolio makes perhaps 100 decisions in any one time period; the impact of any one of the decisions is relatively small, which results in much more breadth and much less volatility than the other two approaches.

These breadth and volatility differences are important in a world where clients are demanding evidence of value-adding skill because the evidence will inevitably be some form of performance attribution analysis generated by clients or their consultants. These constituencies will have more confidence in future returns if a manager can demonstrate an above-average information ratio (value added in relation to volatility, or return/risk). Managers with specific stock-selection ability will find it statistically easier to demonstrate a skill level than industry rotators or market timers.

Figure 7 illustrates the mathematical certainty of this proposition by comparing information ratios (vertical axis) achieved by the three management approaches during a statistically simulated 25-year period. The three managers are assumed to have exactly the same skill level and identical alphas over the long term. The marked differences in information ratios over time have nothing to do with skill but, rather, result from the volatility of outcomes along the way.

Statistically, because the stock picker is making 100 decisions at a time, the stock picker exhibits a good return relative to volatility of return. In fact, the industry rotator would need about six years to achieve the same information ratio a stock picker can achieve in one year. The pure market timer, 100 percent into or out of the market, would likely never get to that level, so a client looking at the market timer's pattern of results would not be able to decide with any confidence whether the manager has skill. This problem is not serious when judging performance after the fact, but it matters a great deal when clients are trying to assess whether future performance is likely to meet their expectations.

Figure 6. Breadth and Volatility: Three Investing Approaches

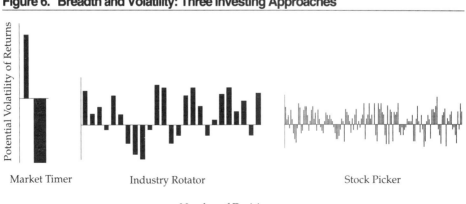

Note: Reward is a function of: Skill level + Number of decisions + Volatility + Time period.

Source: Independence Investment Associates.

Figure 7. Information Ratios (Return/Risk) for Three Investing Approaches

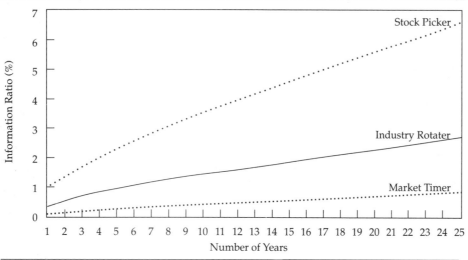

Note: Assumes equal skill levels.

Source: Independence Investment Associates.

Figure 8 converts the information ratios from Figure 7 into *t*-statistics, with the shaded line denoting a *t*-statistic of 2. The figure shows that the stock picker can quickly (in 2 years or less) demonstrate statistical confidence that his or her results are attributable to skill rather than luck and are, therefore, reproducible; the other managers will take longer (5 years for the industry rotator and 17 years for the market timer) to demonstrate skill with the same statistical support.

The mathematical evidence presented in Figures 7 and 8 may explain why fewer and fewer market timers and industry rotators seem to exist as time goes by and why virtually all investment managers now claim to be bottom-up stock pickers. Whether clients and managers are mathematically conscious of it, adding value consistently through stock selection seems inherently easier than adding value through other disciplines; the mathematical results simply reinforce that suspicion.

One of the implications of Figures 7 and 8 is that if a manager's particular skill is industry rotation or market timing, that manager must be much more skillful than the stock picker to produce the same information ratio as a stock picker. **Figure 9** confirms this conclusion. Figure 9's horizontal axis contains the I.C. (skill level) required to produce a 0.50 information ratio, which would be high enough to allow most managers to keep their jobs; the vertical axis measures the number of decisions (breadth) associ-

Figure 8. Reproducibility: *t*-Statistics

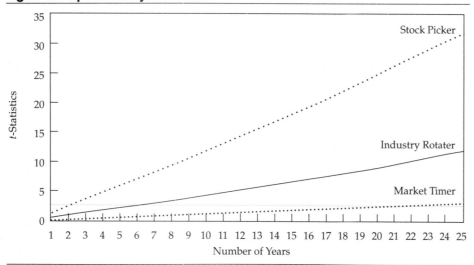

Source: Independence Investment Associates.

Figure 9. Required Skill as a Function of Breadth: I.C. Needed to Produce 0.5 Information Ratio

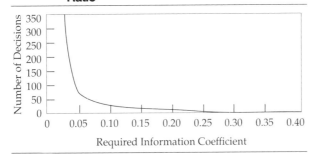

Source: Independence Investment Associates.

Table 1. Performance Attribution

Source	Return	Volatility	Information Ratio
Market timing	–0.03%	0.33%	–0.09%
Style bets	0.61	0.71	0.86
Industry bets	0.23	1.00	0.23
Stock selection	2.40	1.74	1.38
Total active management	3.21%	2.13%	1.51%

Source: Independence Investment Associates.

ated with a given level of I.C. A realistic I.C. for most managers is probably about 0.05, and that coefficient is achieved between 75 and 100 decisions. In other words, making fewer than 75 decisions requires much higher information coefficients to achieve a 0.50 information ratio. As the number of decisions approaches zero, the required information coefficient reaches and exceeds 0.20. The advantage of running a 100-stock portfolio versus a 50-stock portfolio is thus apparent and substantial in terms of the manager's ability to produce consistent results. The skill level needed to rotate in and out of a handful of industries or the market is very high indeed. The inflection point on the required skill level also may help explain the observed tendency over time for managers to structure increasingly diversified portfolios.

Documenting Value-Adding Skills

Some things will not change in a style-neutral world. The timeless necessities for management firms remain the needs to attract talented people, to develop and commit to sensible philosophies, and to serve clients well. But a new lesson must be learned: how to provide documentation to clients of the manager's ability to add long-term value, statistically valid evidence that the manager achieved results through skill that can be reproduced.

Even though formal performance attribution has its critics, it is a tool that can identify for clients, and managers, the particular skills possessed by a given manager. **Table 1** is the performance attribution for a manager that, during the five years ending December 31, 1994, added slightly more than 300 basis points to the benchmark. The most important aspect

is that the manager claimed to be a stock picker and, in fact, most of the return came from stock selection. This manager claimed not to take on much risk (volatility) through industry, factor, or style biases, and the risk column shows that this claim is also true. The manager's actions matched the manager's claims.

This management firm can not only document statistically the high probability of reproducible performance; it also now has the benefit of a value-adding skill (stock picking) that can be transported back and forth across the growth and value realms. Such skill, based on a truly integrated philosophy, allows the manager to outperform the commodity return of a growth, value, or any other benchmark that is within the manager's general sphere of coverage. In effect, the manager has created a "transportable" alpha.

Conclusion

Twenty years ago, value and growth style definitions were not articulated as clearly as they are today. To some extent, perhaps a large extent, the definitions of today are somewhat arbitrary and artificial creations of the pension and consultant communities, and there is no particular reason that these definitions should continue in the future. Indeed, pension fund managers and investment consultants now appear to believe that style distinctions are less important than in the past. In the next decade, growth and value conferences will be replaced by conferences that explore how managers can develop and document reproducible and transportable skills, skills that can add value above and beyond that of a mutually agreed upon benchmark. The value style has historically shown some attractive return characteristics, but clients will pay only for returns in excess of the passive style index.

Stock Valuation and Selection: A Value Investor's Perspective

Edward C. Mitchell, Jr., CFA
Partner and President
INVESCO Capital Management, Inc.

Successful value investing must begin with basic philosophical foundations, then turn to methods of stock valuation and stock selection. A comprehensive value approach also includes portfolio construction processes that recognize and reflect the basic value tenets, and successful value managers follow some clear "do's" and "don'ts."

Volumes of scholarly research and practitioner advice have been written about value investing over the years. This presentation describes the basic approach INVESCO Capital Management has developed and followed during the past 20 or so years. The description begins with some basic philosophical thoughts that form the foundation of the process and then turns to methods of stock valuation, stock selection, and portfolio construction. The presentation closes with a list of do's and don'ts.

Basic Beliefs

Ingrained in our process are certain strongly held beliefs about market efficiency, forecasting, volatility, and the focus of the organization's investment approach and staff.

▪ *Market efficiency.* We believe the markets are efficient, in the sense that security prices reflect the continuous and immediate discounting of new information.

We also believe, however, that the discounting process incorporates investor fears, hopes, forecasts, and expectations about the future that are often incorrect. Therefore, playing the efficient market game is not only worthwhile but can result in victory. As **Figure 1** shows, merely adding 1–2 percent to the market return for a long period of time results in sizable accretions to value.

▪ *Forecasting.* Forecasting is difficult and forms a precarious base for any investment process. The ability to forecast the future accurately and consistently is extremely rare and unlikely to be found in any large investment organization. Furthermore, to be useful, a forecast must not only be correct; it must

also be different from the consensus. Otherwise, it has presumably already been reflected in prices. Unfortunately, any investment process that relies on consistently correct and contrarian forecasts has the odds stacked against it.

Most medium-sized and large companies have certain strongly embedded characteristics that are not subject to frequent or sudden change—for example, brand names, patents, market share, plant and equipment, distribution, management, and financial structure. These aspects do change, but they change only slowly and over long periods of time. Therefore, in analyzing large, well-seasoned companies, the best starting estimate of the future is often an analysis and extrapolation of current and past financial results. This approach is not the most valid for small companies, for which rapid change is common.

▪ *Stock price volatility.* Stock prices are volatile and, in general, are much more volatile than the underlying companies' financial and operating performance. In time, stocks tend to be valued on the basis of earnings and growth rates. The wide price swings that occur in relation to any measure of fair value suggest that investors often forecast more change than actually occurs.

For an illustration, consider the patterns of earnings per share (EPS), book value per share, dividends, and stock price of the example shown in **Figure 2**. The patterns are for a large, well-known pharmaceutical company. The record of rising earnings, dividends, and book value per share—all major determinants of common stock value—is impeccable and unblemished. The stock price, however, although steadily increasing, has experienced substantial fluctuations during short time periods. For most

Figure 1. Winning the Efficient Market Game

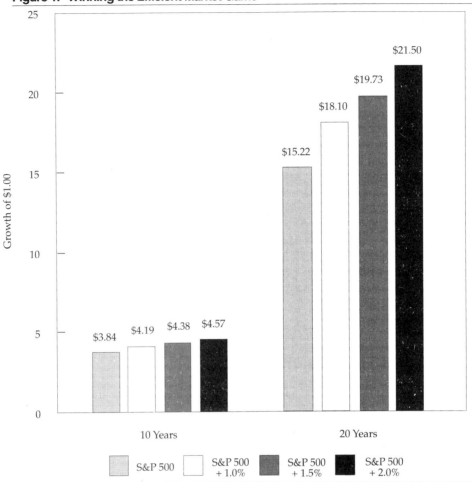

Note: Periods ended December 31, 1994.

Source: INVESCO Capital Management.

companies, this disjunction is not at all unusual, as evidenced by a simple comparison of the spreads between the yearly high and low prices of virtually all actively traded common stocks.

▨ *Investment discipline and implementation.* With a disciplined process of stock selection and an emphasis on risk control in the portfolio structure, investment portfolios can be constructed that produce incremental returns to the market return with less than market risk. The probability for success of an investment organization is measurably enhanced by having a stable group of well-trained, experienced professionals who are willing to work cooperatively in support of that common investment discipline.

Investment Process

The INVESCO investment process evolved during the late 1960s and early 1970s. Many of us came into the business about this time and have spent our entire investment careers together. Key to our development was early and strong commitment to the CFA® program, which introduced us to and immersed us in a growing and accepted "body of knowledge" related to financial and security analysis.

As we struggled to develop a rational investment process, we were heavily influenced by the writings and research associated with the concepts of modern portfolio theory. From the pioneers, we gained substantial insights into methods of security valuation and ways of measuring and controlling portfolio risk.

Ultimately, however, the investment process that emerged, and continues to develop, was based on the practical application of stock market theory—application based on our individual and collective experiences and learned through trial and error.

Relative Stock Valuation

Accepted criteria for selecting value stocks generally include a low price relative to earnings, dividends, book value, replacement cost, break-up value, cash flow, or net working capital per share. Often, these

Figure 2. Pharmaceutical Company Fundamentals and Price

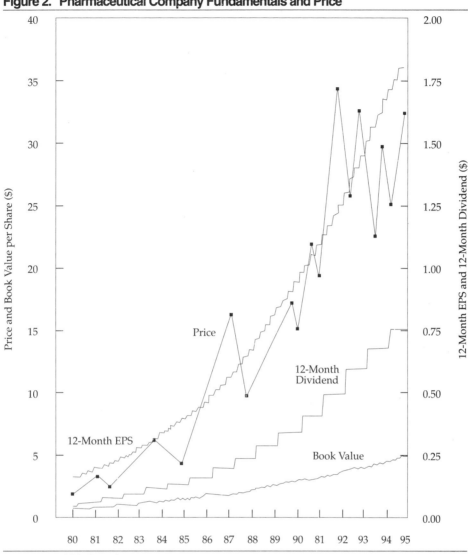

Source: INVESCO Capital Management.

criteria are the primary bases for stock selection. INVESCO's approach is somewhat different; although the criteria ultimately characterize our value portfolios, they are not the initial criteria.

The cornerstone of our stock valuation methodology is the basic concept underlying the dividend discount model: Simply put, the worth of a company is equal to the present value of future dividends—in the words of Molodovsky, "the hard core of stock values."

The Dividend Discount Model

The DDM states that the present value (*PV*) of the company is equal to the sum of all the expected future dividends ($D_1, ..., D_n$), divided by the difference between the investors' required rate of return (*k*) and the expected growth rate (*g*):

$$PV = \frac{D_1}{(1+k)^1} + \frac{D_2}{(1+k)^2} + \frac{D_3}{(1+k)^3} + ... + \frac{(D_{n+1})/(k-g)}{(1+k)^n}.$$

The model may be more familiar in the form:

$$PV = \frac{D_1}{k-g}.$$

Most investment professionals would agree on the theoretical soundness of the DDM, but its practical application entails overcoming legitimate hurdles. Most significant is the difficulty of precisely estimating future growth rates for an extended period of time. Anyone who has ever worked with a DDM knows that even small changes in growth rates produce large changes in fair value.

Valuation Approach

To address that difficulty, INVESCO's application of the DDM does not require the subjective estimation of future growth rates for hundreds of companies. Instead, we start with the demonstrated historical record of each company and ask four questions, the first two of which directly address the growth issue:

- What does the company earn?
- How much does the company reinvest?
- How much risk does the company take?
- What is the current price of the stock?

The columns in **Table 1** identify the elements of our valuation process as we attempt to answer those questions.

Because our universe consists of medium-sized and large companies, the companies have enough history and maturity to have meaningful records and we have sufficient data on each company to follow this valuation approach. Our process also assumes that, in time, each company's return on equity (ROE) and payout ratio will revert to the long-term average for U.S. industry. Classical economic theory teaches that abnormally high profit margins cannot persist and will eventually be competed away. On the other hand, companies with a history of poor performance should, in time, either improve their profitability or fade away.

Given these data and assumptions, we set out to answer the four questions. We know what the company has earned on shareholders' equity on a normalized basis (normalizing involves weighing several observations, with more weight given to recent results in order to reflect evolutionary changes in profitability). We know what the "normal" payout ratio is—how much is paid out in dividends and how much is reinvested. Normalized ROE times normalized earnings retention yields a normalized growth rate, which we then use for g in the DDM.

With this g and the known current price and book value, we have all the information we need to calculate the figure for the "expected return" column of Table 1 (or, in the parlance of the DDM, to solve for k) and to do so without being required to make specific forecasts about future growth rates.

Table 1 also includes columns for "risk adjustment" and "adjusted expected return." We modify the DDM results by the risk-adjustment factor to adjust expected returns upward for companies that take relatively less risk and downward for those that take more risk. The risk-adjustment factor reflects both operating risk, as measured by earnings stability, and financial risk, as measured by cash flow coverage of fixed charges. The maximum adjustment made to the calculated expected return k is 2 percentage points. The greatest emphasis is on earnings stability, which measures the volatility of a company's historical ROE. The financial risk component is the traditional calculation of interest coverage ([Pretax income + Depreciation + Interest]/Interest).

Example of Relative Valuation

For an illustration of how the valuation process works, compare the figures in Table 1 for the pharmaceutical company and the electric utility company. The 1993 data indicate that the pharmaceutical company is a highly profitable operation, as measured by ROE, that is able to reinvest a substantial portion (61 percent) of its earnings at that high ROE rate. Even if this company's profitability and reinvestment rate were to decline to average over time, the implied high earnings and dividend growth discounted by the current price would yield a large expected rate of return. When adjusted for risk, the return only improves; the balance sheet is strong, and the earnings very stable. When risk and return are combined, the stock ranks in the fifth percentile, more attractive than 95 percent of the other stocks in our universe.

Contrast that picture with the electric utility. Returns for the utility in 1993 are average to below average, and nearly all the earnings are paid out. (By the way, this high payout ratio is actually beneficial from the shareholder's perspective. Low-return companies should pay out their earnings to owners, rather than reinvest them in the companies' current low-re-

Table 1. Relative Stock Valuations

Company	Price per Share	Book Value per Share	Return on Equity	Payout Ratio	Expected Return	Cash Flow Coverage of Fixed Charges	Earnings Stability	Risk-Adjust-ment Factor	Adjusted Expected Return	Percentile Rank
December 31, 1993										
Pharmaceutical	$29.63	$ 4.35	36.0%	39%	17.30%	20.00×	0.872	1.52%	18.82%	4.8
Electric utility	47.63	25.47	12.2	89	8.56	3.63	0.749	0.05	8.62	73.7
December 31, 1994										
Pharmaceutical	32.63	4.91	36.0	39	17.46	20.00	0.873	1.52	18.98	5.2
Electric utility	35.63	26.36	12.1	90	10.57	3.92	0.748	0.06	10.63	57.8

Source: INVESCO Capital Management.

turn operations, to allow the owners to invest in higher return opportunities.) The valuation process makes little or no adjustment for risk, and this unattractive stock ranks in the 74th percentile. In essence, the extremely low reinvestment rate and low level of profitability more than offset the company's low stock price relative to its potential future value.

One year later, book values have risen slightly for both companies, but returns, payouts, and risk profiles are essentially the same. Only the stock prices are different. The pharmaceutical stock price is up 10 percent but with little effect on its relative ranking; the electric utility stock has fallen by 25 percent, causing its percentile rank to improve from unattractive to neutral.

Pharmaceutical stock is normally considered a classic growth stock. Certainly, it does not fit the conventional definition of a value stock—low P/E, high yield, low price to book value (P/B). If the pharmaceutical company's record is a reasonably close approximation of its future returns, however, even after allowing for gradually diminishing profitability over time, we would conclude that this company is relatively undervalued. Utilities, on the other hand, with their high yields, low P/Es, and low P/Bs, tend to resemble value stocks, but this methodology indicates that, at the current price, this utility stock is not undervalued.

This example raises the issue that the methodology and its conclusions can be confusing. Consultants, and even our clients, often remark that INVESCO does not fit the model of a traditional value manager. Our response is that whether we fit the model depends on the definition of value. Our definition, incorporating the four questions set forth earlier, is unique to INVESCO and considers a company's historical profitability versus its current price in determining relative valuation as opposed to evaluating only the single-point-in-time characteristics of current P/E, yield, or P/B.

Stock Selection

After the universe has been ranked by relative value through the process outlined in Table 1, we narrow the field of potential investment candidates to the best one-third in the universe. The next step is more difficult, more subjective and judgmental, and more time-consuming than the valuation part of the process. Rather than the purely quantitative method outlined previously, it involves an in-depth analysis of each company's embedded characteristics, environment, business strategy, and resources.

Because we initially value companies on the basis of their records, the key question in step two becomes: Is the historical record still relevant or has

a significant change occurred in the company, its industry, or the environment that would lead to the conclusion that the record is no longer very useful for valuation purposes? We attempt to answer this question through our own internal research process, which uses information from many outside sources, including company contacts, third-party research, data-base services, and Wall Street. Our focus is long-term analysis; we have little use for research concentrated on the near term, such as the short-term earnings forecasts that pervade Wall Street. We do, however, use the Street's corps of experienced and highly skilled analysts to help us understand company and industry fundamentals.

The result of this analysis is a list of purchase candidates—companies that are (1) relatively undervalued based on price and record, (2) ranked in the top third of our universe, and (3) have records we believe are reasonable estimates of future growth and profitability. **Exhibit 1** contains an example for the pharmaceutical company depicted in Table 1.

Exhibit 1. Pharmaceutical Company Analysis

Quantitative Valuation
    Ranks in the top 5 percent of our universe based on its
        historical record.
Qualitative Corporate Analysis
- Worldwide leader with strong brand positions in pharmaceuticals, hospital supplies/equipment, and over-the-counter products.
- Consistent long-term operating performance.
- Diversified product line.
- Financially powerful with little debt and strong cash flow.
- Sizable commitments to research and development.
- Competitive pricing advantages because of size and business mix.
- Focused on new-product introductions, new indications on existing products, and cost-effective solutions to health care providers.

Conclusion
    Pharmaceutical company's past record and fundamental
        characteristics justify purchase at current prices.

Portfolio Construction

From our selected list, portfolios are statistically constructed and monitored through the use of a computer-based risk-estimation model. Our objectives are to

- maximize the use of the best ranked stocks based on our valuation criteria;
- control portfolio risk (portfolios have high R^2s and low standard errors); and
- control turnover through a clearly established sell discipline.

The sell discipline consists of three mandates. First, a stock is sold when it becomes statistically overvalued and falls into the bottom 15 percent of our universe. This development can happen for two reasons: The stock's price may rise dramatically, thereby reducing its expected return, or the inputs to our model for the company (book value, ROE, payout ratio) may change significantly because of some corporate action, such as a merger, acquisition, stock repurchase, or other operating results.

The sell discipline avoids the greatest single risk in investing: paying up for a forecast. Stock prices often rise in anticipation of some dramatic upswing in future earnings; the anticipation is based on forecasted cyclical or secular changes that may or may not take place, however, for one, two, or even several years. If a stock's rank falls into the bottom 15 percent for this reason, then we are unwilling to take the additional risk that these forecasts will not be realized.

The second mandate is that stocks be sold when a portfolio's overall rank declines below the targeted level of the 30th percentile. Marginally ranked equities are reduced in size or eliminated so that the proceeds can be reinvested in better ranked stocks. The third mandate is that a stock be sold when its corporate analysis changes (or proves to be wrong) as a result of some material change in the company or its environment.

This stock selection process, even with a rigorous sell discipline, is flexible enough to allow evaluation of all companies in the same manner and is not tied to any narrowly constrained definition of value. **Figure 3** provides a representative example of this construction process in action; it compares a sample INVESCO portfolio with the S&P 500 Index as of December 1994. Figure 3 suggests that our somewhat different approach (reflecting our definition of value and emphasis on the DDM) results in a portfolio that would meet the criteria of most value managers. For example, the dividend yield, P/E, and P/B relative to the S&P 500 are all indicative of a conventional value portfolio.

Do's and Don'ts

INVESCO's guidelines to stock valuation and selection, portfolio construction, and client service may belabor the obvious, but because they are based on 25 years of experience, they are worth noting.

- *Do*
  - Have a discipline and stick to it.
  - Diversify and control risk.
  - Be patient and stay oriented toward the long term.
  - Trade only when there is a compelling reason.
  - Have realistic performance expectations.
  - Provide a high level of client service.
- *Don't*
  - Act on emotion or change strategy in midstream.
  - Make big bets.
  - Try to time the market or focus on the short term.
  - Churn or have unnecessarily high turnover.
  - Promise more than you can deliver on performance.
  - Forget to communicate with clients in writing, by phone, and in person.

Finally, efforts to invest sensibly and with discipline for the long term will not only be justified; they will add value. Small incremental additions to the market return over time make playing the so-called efficient market game worthwhile and even a winnable venture.

Figure 3. Representative Portfolio versus the S&P 500, as of December 31, 1994

Risk Profile

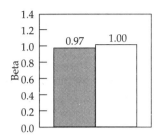

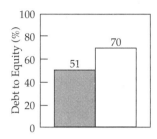

Valuation

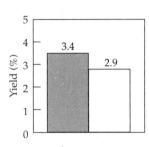

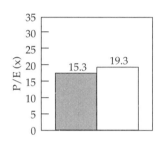

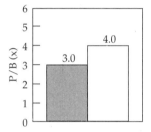

Profitability

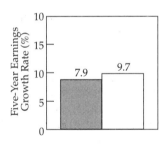

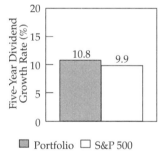

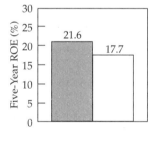

■ Portfolio □ S&P 500

Source: INVESCO Capital Management.

The Advantage to Value Investing

Lewis A. Sanders, CFA
Chairman and CEO
Sanford C. Bernstein and Company, Inc.

Value investing produces above-average returns that are enduring and available globally. Two behavioral axioms—(1) value equals anxiety and (2) reversion to the mean—underlie the performance of value investing. Empirical evidence in the United States and other developed markets attests to the veracity of the axioms and to the level of the performance.

Proponents of any investment style must base their strategies on certain essential propositions. This presentation assumes three major propositions about value investing. First, it is efficacious. Buying earnings power, dividends, and assets for a price that is low compared with the standards of the day is very likely to produce a risk-adjusted return that is well above average. Second, value anomalies are outgrowths of behavioral, as opposed to financial, phenomena. Thus, the above-average returns produced by those anomalies will prove enduring, not because they are particularly difficult to identify or to capture, but because life in the value domain is fundamentally distasteful and will be avoided by many investors. Third, and most important, the value style in the United States applies equally well to all capital markets of the developed world and for precisely the same reasons. Despite cultural differences, the behavioral factors that drive the value style in the United States are manifest globally. The presentation develops two axioms that underlie these propositions and examines empirical findings that illustrate the axioms and make the case for an advantage to value investing.

Biases about Wealth Management

Both introspection and focused observation suggest that some common biases are apparent in wealth management, and these biases work to the benefit of value investing.

   Overvaluation of certainty. People seem to have an overwhelming affection for things that are or appear to be certain. They like them so much that they consistently overbuy them and overpay for them. Household financial wealth, for example, is dominated by assets, such as money market funds, that have very low or no perceived volatility—even when volatility should not make a difference, and at the sacrifice of considerable long-term return.

   Overreaction to big, unlikely, but consequential events. People are attracted to such events when the consequences of winning seem magnificent, even when they logically know the chances of winning are very small. This tendency explains the popularity of lotteries. In the financial markets, this behavioral bias fuels many financing and investing binges. Indeed, whole industries have been financed as a function of this behavioral bias; the most recent significant example is biotechnology.

   Loss aversion. In people's minds, fear of losses looms considerably larger than expectation of gains. For most, the pain of a loss significantly exceeds the pleasure of an equivalent gain.

Derived from real-world experiments performed by behavioral scientists Kahneman and Tversky, **Figure 1** depicts the value that people assign gains and losses. In the domain of potential losses, the slope of the line steepens sharply. The message is clear: People do not like losses. The only thing they dislike more than losing money is the investment managers who lose it for them.

Value = Anxiety

These behavioral biases underlie the first of the two major axioms of value investing, namely, that value equals anxiety. That is, anxiety-producing capital assets—those framed in the domain of potential losses—will be priced to offer returns that are meaningfully higher than the returns justified by the actual risks taken. Assets in this domain typically do

Figure 1. Loss Aversion

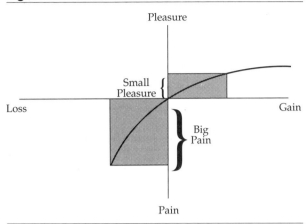

Source: Sanford C. Bernstein and Co., based on Amos Tversky and Daniel Kahneman, "Rational Choice and the Framing of Decisions," *The Journal of Business*, No. 4 (1986).

not achieve that status overnight; rather, they earn it by first persistently disappointing anyone who has been willing to invest in them. If the pattern of disappointment keeps up long enough, the reaction turns to disgust. If the pattern goes on still longer, if it attracts attention, if it becomes the subject of persistent negative media coverage, and in the extreme, if ownership carries serious risks to the owner's reputation, the disgust turns to despair and, ultimately, fear. Accordingly, value anomalies are almost always outgrowths of progressive discouragement, and given loss aversion, assets subject to this process should and do eventually provide disproportionately high returns. The behavioral basis for this phenomenon also suggests that these results should be observed in most, if not all, developed markets.

United States

The impact on U.S. stock returns of changing investor expectations substantiates that value anomalies are generated by progressive discouragement and do produce above-average returns. **Figure 2** plots the return impact on stocks in the S&P 500 Index of changing expectations for near-term earnings—specifically, 12-month earnings forecasts—during the 20-year period ending in 1993. Changing expectations are reflected in either positive or negative earnings revisions, and the frequency bars indicate the number of incidences of both types of revisions, grouped by size. The leftward preponderance of frequency bars indicates more downward revisions than upward, which reflects the perennially optimistic positions that analysts take. The effects of these expectational shifts on relative returns are large, from +300 to –200 basis points (bps) versus the S&P 500, and take time to filter through to valu-

Figure 2. Impact of Expectational Shifts: S&P 500 Returns

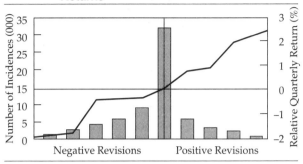

Source: Sanford C. Bernstein and Co., based on data from Institutional Broker's Estimate System (IBES).

ation. In fact, these performance premiums and penalties were measured for the period three months after the expectational shifts were observed. Stable expectations are neither rewarded nor penalized; no relative return is associated with the "no earnings revisions" frequency bar. But for upward and downward revisions, the relative performance response is basically monotonic; that is, the larger the revisions, the larger the relative performance effect.

Significantly, the downward revisions are highly serially correlated; that is, as **Figure 3** reveals, the probability is very high that a stock that has already

Figure 3. Serially Correlated Negative Revisions: S&P 500 Returns

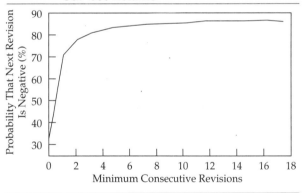

Source: Sanford C. Bernstein and Co.

experienced one or more downward revisions will experience additional downward revision. These data reinforce something investment managers know from experience: People do not adjust to events all at once. Their first reactions to deterioration are almost always inadequate, so they are likely to generate additional downward revisions. This common behavioral bias is known as "anchoring."

U.S. stock prices respond dramatically to progressive discouragement, as illustrated in **Figure 4**. Performance penalties increase as discouragement builds for the first six or seven of these revisions.

Figure 4. Performance Impact of Negative
Revisions: S&P 500 Returns

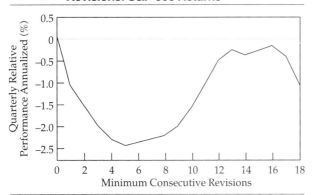

Source: Sanford C. Bernstein and Co.

After many such revisions, a curious phenomenon occurs: The incremental performance penalties begin to subside. Could a countervailing effect be surfacing? Perhaps value investors are beginning to find these stocks "cheap" and buy into the bad news, moderating its effects.

Figure 5 repeats the analysis shown in Figure 2 for a subset of stocks deemed cheap, as defined by traditional value investing metrics—price-to-book-

Figure 5. Impact of Expectational Shifts: Cheap
S&P 500 Stocks

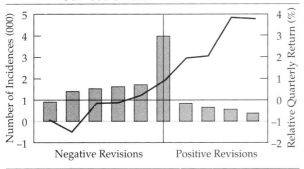

Source: Sanford C. Bernstein and Co., based on data from IBES.

value ratios, price-to-earnings ratios, and relative dividend yield. This subset is evidently the domain of discouragement; the stocks in this subset are dominated by downward revisions. What is particularly interesting about this apparently gloomy environment is that the performance penalties associated with more disappointment diminish. Indeed, the returns in this group of stocks actually become positive (nearly 100 bps) in the mere presence of stability (no revisions) in expectations.

Figure 5 depicts a high-return domain, but the selling of these stocks can be thought of as paying the buyers to endure the stress of ownership that the sellers can no longer take. For example, consider buying housing stocks in 1982 with mortgage rates

at 17 percent, or various auto and steel stocks in the Rust Belt era of the 1980s, oil stocks in 1986 when the price crashed from $25 to $10 a barrel, or financial stocks in the early 1990s—a value theme involving the most extreme form of ownership stress. This use of the seller's money is certainly fair, but it places the value manager, for all practical purposes, in a psychiatric role. The domain of discouragement is not for the timid, and value managers must be up to the challenge of pursuing what is uncomfortable. As a group, they often fail to beat benchmarks at the most critical times simply because life in this domain just before the moment of payoff can be extremely difficult to negotiate—in fact, so difficult that many managers cannot or will not stay the course.

The opposite kind of emotional state applies at the other end of the value spectrum—the subset of "expensive" stocks according to the value metrics. **Figure 6** depicts the domain of presumed predictability, stability in earnings. People prize this stability; it makes them feel secure, and they are willing to

Figure 6. Impact of Expectational Shifts: Expensive
S&P 500 Stocks

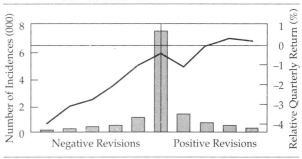

Source: Sanford C. Bernstein and Co., based on data from IBES.

pay to feel secure. In contrast to the no-return case in Figure 2 and the positive-return case in Figure 5, stable expectations in Figure 6 actually generate a negative return—roughly 50 bps. At the same time, the penalties for any disappointment are severe indeed—a drop in returns of as much as 400 bps. Moreover, the benefits of positive revisions are surprisingly scant. After all, the price is already very high.

The contrasts between Figures 2 and 6 and Figure 5 clearly demonstrate, for the United States, the validity of the first axiom: Pain and suffering are rewarded in the capital markets.

International

Performing a similar analysis for the rest of the developed world is difficult because the available data are limited and their statistical relevance is questionable. The data that are available, however, are persuasive. **Figure 7** compares the reactions in

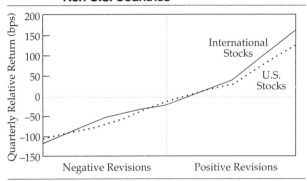

Figure 7. International Impact of Expectational Shifts: U.S. Stocks and Stocks of Ten Non-U.S. Countries

Source: Sanford C. Bernstein and Co., based on data from IBES and MSCI.

the United States with investor reactions to revisions of short-run expectations (revisions of 12-month earnings expectations measured 3 months after the fact) for ten developed countries: Australia, Canada, France, Germany, Hong Kong, Italy, Japan, the Netherlands, Switzerland, and the United Kingdom. The index was a capitalization-weighted intersection of the Institutional Broker's Estimate System (IBES) and Morgan Stanley Capital International (MSCI) universes. The figure incorporates only six to seven years (1987–93) of data for the international markets, but the lines show that investor response to changing expectations in these markets is remarkably similar to the U.S. experience, especially the absence of any return associated with stable expectations.

Figure 8 portrays investor response in the domain of cheap stocks from Figure 7, and **Figure 9** presents the same analysis for expensive stocks, with the same value metrics applied to delineate the subsets. These figures carry the same message that held in the U.S. case: Higher returns accrue when discouragement is high, and lower returns are associated with predictability. Although not conclusive, the

Figure 8. Impact of Expectational Shifts: Cheap Stocks of International Companies and the United States

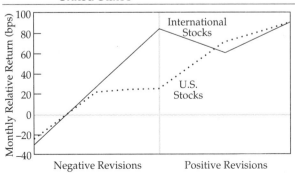

Source: Sanford C. Bernstein and Co., based on data from IBES and MSCI.

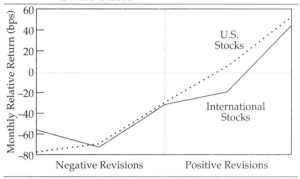

Figure 9. Impact of Expectational Shifts: Expensive Stocks of International Companies and the United States

Source: Sanford C. Bernstein and Co., based on data from IBES and MSCI.

data strongly suggest that non-U.S. investors are moved by short-run earnings disappointments in a manner analogous to the behavior of U.S. investors. If anything, the relative rewards and penalties are even more pronounced internationally.

Mean Reversion

The behavioral loop is not yet closed. Identifying the process by which value anomalies are generated—progressive discouragement—does not address how those anomalies are ultimately resolved. The second axiom of value investing addresses this issue and is popularly known as mean reversion: Good things get worse; bad things get better.

Figure 10 shows quintiles ranked from highest to lowest based on corporate return on equity (ROE) for approximately 1,000 U.S. companies within ± 2 bps of market capitalization for the 1963–92 period. The initial rankings reflect how well the companies were doing at the beginning of the period, not the prices of the stocks. The graph traces the quintile ROEs during the next five years. What the lines

Figure 10. Return on Equity: 1,000 U.S. Companies by Quintiles, 1963–92

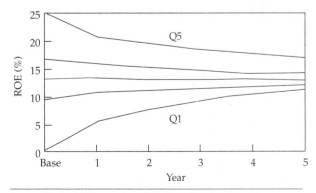

Source: Sanford C. Bernstein and Co., based on data from Compustat.

reveal is the strong tendency for ROEs to regress to the mean from both directions. **Figure 11**, for a subset of 800 companies in the MSCI universe from 1975 through 1992, suggests that mean reversion is a global phenomenon; the same tendency for ROEs to converge is evident in non-U.S. companies. **Figure 12**

Figure 11. Return on Equity: Non-U.S. Companies by Quintiles, 1975–93

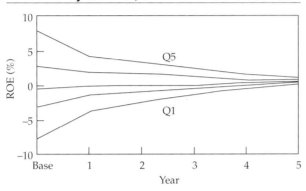

Source: Sanford C. Bernstein and Co., based on data from MSCI.

provides market-specific evidence of mean reversion for four developed markets. That value-oriented strategies produce superior returns in these markets as well as in the U.S. market should be no surprise.

These results reflect another facet of human behavior: Success has a strong tendency to attract emulators and, sometimes, to breed complacency and conservatism on the part of the successful. This phenomenon leaves the high-return companies vulnerable to erosion in profitability. Tough times cause the opposite kind of response; capital tends to flee, and corporate managers rise to the occasion with initiatives to turn the tide. If they do not, new managers will. In time, therefore, more often than not, the tide does turn.

The Global Value Investor's Advantage

Because the behavioral biases for return differences seem to hold across developed markets, value investors should have an advantage across markets. **Figure 13** suggests that they do. Figure 13 shows the relative performance (premium or deficit) of value investing to the GDP-weighted benchmark for the ten developed non-U.S. markets shown in Figures 7–9 for the past 20 years. Value investing earned a premium relative to the benchmark about 75 percent of the time, and the premiums were often quite high.

Figure 14 summarizes 14 years of value stock performance, relative to the appropriate MSCI country benchmark, for five of the major countries of the ten shown in Figure 13 plus the United States. In every case, value outperformed the benchmark—in some cases, by as much as 500 bps.

The evidence strongly suggests that the pain of uncertainty, the difficulty of living in the domain of discouragement, and the inevitability of mean rever-

Figure 12. Return on Equity: Four Largest Non-U.S. Developed Economies

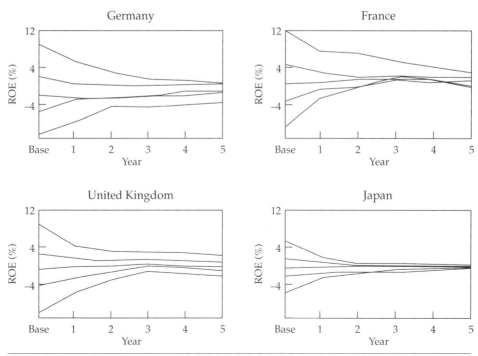

Source: Sanford C. Bernstein and Co., based on data from MSCI.

Figure 13. Value Performance: Ten Non-U.S. Developed Countries

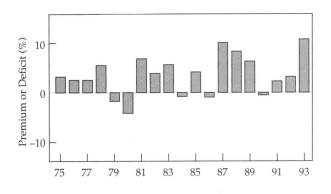

Source: Sanford C. Bernstein and Co., based on data from MSCI.

Figure 14. Annualized Returns for Value Investing versus Country Benchmarks: Six Developed Countries, 1980–93

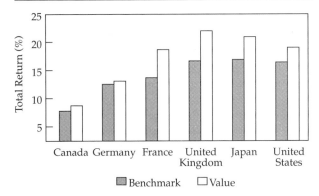

Note: Return defined as total return in local currency, net dividends.

Source: Sanford C. Bernstein and Co., based on data from MSCI.

sion are as profitable in developed world countries as they are in the United States. The behavioral basis for this phenomenon is more or less universal.

The returns to value are not well correlated geo-graphically, however, which is significant. In fact, the correlations between countries, shown in **Table 1**, are approximately zero. Value anomalies occur in different intensities, in different industries, and at different times in these countries. The underlying lack of synchronization of the world economies means that the anomalies pay off asynchronously. Today, for instance, the United States is booming—in terms of both growth and corporate profitability. Japan, which has hardly emerged from recession, has a richly priced currency that puts tremendous pressure on its corporate sector and has extremely depressed profitability. One would expect the profiles of investor stress to be different in the two countries, and the value anomalies are, indeed, different.

The lack of country correlations confers an important diversification benefit, as shown in **Table 2**. The volatility of returns to a value strategy concurrently used in ten countries—in this case, GDP weighted—is far less than that of any single country in the same group. The need for style diversification is typically thought of as combining value and growth styles in a single geography to dampen the volatility of returns to active management. Table 2

Table 2. Returns to Non-U.S. Value Investing, 1980–93

	Total Relative Return[a]	Best Year	Worst Year	Standard Deviation
Ten-country strategy	3.3%	11.1%	–4.5%	4.0%
Japan	6.1	16.8	–7.0	5.5
Germany	2.8	17.8	–4.7	5.4
France	4.0	19.0	–10.8	6.7
United Kingdom	2.3	21.0	–14.4	9.2

[a]Total relative return versus local benchmark.

Source: Sanford C. Bernstein and Co., based on data from MSCI.

Table 1. Correlations of Value Returns: Six Largest Developed Non-U.S. Economies, 1975–93

Country	Canada	France	Germany	Italy	Japan	United Kingdom
Canada	1.0	0.2	0.2	0.0	0.1	0.2
France		1.0	0.2	–0.1	–0.1	0.4
Germany			1.0	0.1	0.2	0.0
Italy				1.0	0.1	–0.1
Japan					1.0	0.0
United Kingdom						1.0

Note: Correlations are dollar based.

Source: Sanford C. Bernstein and Co., based on data from MSCI.

suggests that an equally efficacious, although not mutually exclusive, approach is to diversify the value style geographically.

Conclusion

The principal dynamics in the world's capital markets revolve around a tug-of-war between feeling secure and making money. In the end, the feelings generally win out. A substantial amount of money can thus be made if a value investment manager is willing to spend the bulk of his or her professional life feeling depressed, isolated, and afraid, waiting for the forces of mean reversion to relieve the stress, at which point the manager will sell and use the proceeds to rebuild anxiety. Is it worth it? This question, of course, is philosophical, but the money on the table is considerable, and the question deserves serious thought.

Question and Answer Session: Value

Stanford Calderwood
William C. Fletcher, CFA
Edward C. Mitchell, Jr., CFA
Lewis A. Sanders, CFA

Question: Please describe your sell discipline.

Sanders: Most value managers approach security selection with some kind of scoring system, some rank ordering of the universe of securities from which they select. If, by definition, high-ranked securities are purchase candidates and low-ranked securities are noncandidates, a natural sell discipline evolves as securities fall to the middle of the universe rankings or below. A scoring system implies a natural migration as securities progress through the value or investment cycle and rise and fall in rank, ultimately being replaced as they change from being undervalued to being fairly valued.

Mitchell: The only hard-and-fast rule in our firm is to sell stocks that are statistically overvalued, although doing so sometimes means leaving money on the table. When a stock becomes overvalued according to our statistical approach, one (or both) of two things, neither good, has happened—the stock's price relative to other stocks in the universe has risen dramatically, or the company's absolute profitability has declined precipitously.

Beyond this strict rule, we also control the portfolio by weighting all the stocks in the portfolio by their respective ranks in the universe and selling whenever the portfolio's overall rank falls below the 30th percentile. This practice creates continual refreshing as stocks fall in rank, are sold, and are replaced by stocks whose rankings have risen.

Fletcher: Our ranking system is not symmetrical; the lowest ranked stocks underperform by a larger margin than the highest ranked stocks outperform. As at least a partial consequence of this observation, the only time we trade a portfolio is if a stock needs to be sold; we never trade because we want to buy a stock. If we did nothing other than own the S&P 500 Index and avoid the bottom-ranked stocks, we would achieve our clients' performance objectives. Obviously, we spend a lot of time identifying attractively priced stocks that maintain the risk profile of the portfolio, but we believe we have more skill in avoiding the losers than in making the big bets.

Calderwood: Using eight valuation models, we rank a universe of stocks and create a composite scoring system in which a stock is a mandatory "sell" the moment it reaches the eighth or lower decile. Very few stocks are actually sold by this rule, however, because stocks that are bought as "buy" ranked (the top three deciles) generally don't suddenly become sell ranked. They tend to drift down through the "hold" deciles (fourth through seventh) and to be sold off and replaced by a buy-ranked stock before they reach the sell zone.

We also have a statistical model that seems to be especially prescient in identifying tenth decile stocks. When that model gives a sell signal, we tend to believe it regardless of what our other disciplines are telling us.

Question: What is your intended and actual turnover?

Calderwood: Our turnover is a function of our stock rankings. For the last decade, turnover has averaged 50–60 percent, but it can vary. In some market conditions, the market takes longer to recognize what our models have identified as undervalued stocks and our turnover drops. In other conditions, the market recognizes undervalued stocks quickly, prices go up, and stocks on the buy list are replaced by other stocks, which increases turnover. Turnover is generally low when the value style is out of favor and the market's attention is primarily on growth stocks.

Question: What is your view on holding cash?

Mitchell: We do not emphasize market timing. We do a modest amount of cash allocation, however, primarily to control risk. We establish the allocation based on a proven set of relationships between the expected return from stocks and current interest rates. The last time we had any material amounts of cash would have been during pre-crash 1987, a time of both rapidly rising stock prices and interest rates. The risk–reward relationship between stocks and their alternatives was not very promising, and we had a 20–25 percent cash allocation.

Question: If value investing is so good, why are there so few value managers?

Sanders: That question gets at the very essence of value investing. Value investing at its most extreme is intensely distasteful. What defines value is highly correlated with unpopularity, and by that definition, return premiums derive from distasteful commitments and positions. One way to think about the capital markets is that risk premiums are distributed across various assets in various geographies, with the highest risk premiums and returns located where the anxiety and tension are highest. So, why would we expect to find a multitude of true value managers? Many managers wear the value label, but not many truly practice the discipline; it is very difficult to stay in the kitchen when the heat is turned up.

Question: In a style-neutral context, how do you avoid being all things to all people?

Fletcher: First, the manager has to separate in his or her mind the commodity part of return, the part available through a style benchmark, from the value that can be added, which is available through whatever skills the manager brings to the process. Consequently, the question of managing two such very different benchmarks as value and growth becomes a question of having a value-adding "engine," a skill set that can be applied in either setting.

Personally, I would not want an organization that did two completely different things—with totally different philosophies, research departments, and portfolios. We have one research group following the same stock universe using the same valuation ranking system; the only separation comes when we engineer a portfolio structure that has either value or growth characteristics. The active positions in those portfolios are identical. In one portfolio, we may have 40 percent in financial institutions' stocks versus a benchmark of 35 percent, and in another portfolio, 10 percent in financials versus a 5 percent benchmark. In either case, the active bet is driven by the same skill set and simply overlaid on the underlying commodity portfolio characteristics.

The Security Analyst's Changing Role

Patrick O'Donnell
Managing Director and Director of Equity Research
Putnam Investments

As greater professionalism attaches to the role of security analysts, increased attention is being paid to nurturing analysts' creativity and imagination. These changes have had profound effects on the investment industry and will continue to pose daunting but rewarding challenges to money managers and people managers.

Two major themes, which are already evident in some investing institutions, will characterize the next decade in investment analysis, in my opinion. The first is a new professionalism in the job of the securities analyst, including opportunities for career analysts to play much larger roles than previously in investment decisions. The second theme is increased attention to the professional management of research departments and, in order to improve investment results, to helping analysts stay creative and imaginative throughout their careers.

This presentation focuses on the changes, in the industry and the profession, that underlie these two themes. It is an attempt to predict some of the ways those changes will unfold in the future and what the changes mean for the day-to-day challenge of managing groups of creative people who are responsible for large amounts of other people's money.

A Brief Review (with Numbers That Tell Only Part of the Tale)

The money-management business has grown tremendously in the past 20 years. From 1975 to the end of 1994, assets under professional management grew from about $750 billion to about $9.1 trillion, a compound growth rate of 14 percent for two decades. During this period, mutual fund assets grew at a 23 percent compound annual rate (to $2.1 trillion) while retirement fund assets compounded at a 14 percent rate (to $6.2 trillion). A particularly interesting statistic is the increasing concentration of mutual fund assets during the last decade. I will return to this topic later, but for now, note that 5 percent of mutual fund managers now have 63 percent of mutual fund assets. Incremental cash flows are going to fewer and fewer managers.

The number of people involved in the money-management business has also grown substantially during this period, although at a somewhat slower pace than the growth of assets under management. Since 1974, membership in AIMR has increased from 12,679 to 28,587, a compound growth rate of 4.2 percent. The number of professional money-management firms has grown even faster, from 638 in about 1975 to 2,176 now, a growth rate of 6.4 percent a year.

The statistics reveal the dimensions of the money-management business and its wonderful growth, but they reveal little about the state of professional practice or the ways it has changed over the years. The progress that has been made in many areas notwithstanding, I have the sense that less research and, in particular, less high-quality, fundamental research and analysis is occurring now than before the bull market took off in 1982. I cannot prove this observation by citing numbers because no statistics show what investment professionals do all day long. I can say, however, that my own informal poll of a wide range of investment professionals with long experience in the business found universal agreement that company-specific, bottom-up research is actually done much less frequently than is claimed.

Industry observers cite a number of causes for this de-emphasis on fundamental research, including the proliferation of so-called passive or market-indexed investing approaches and the shrinking of many formerly large research departments because of either greater reliance on quantitative methods of portfolio construction or reduced staff resulting from cost cutting, which is sometimes driven by industry consolidation. The growth in the 1980s of small firms that lacked the resources to do independent research may be another factor. The most cynical industry experts suggest that in a bull market, fundamental research is less important than the marketing and distribution of both institutional products and mutual funds.

The quantitative revolution's footprints—and benefits—are everywhere in the industry. At Putnam Investments, we recently undertook a literature search of everything written about securities analysis since 1980. The search disclosed that the overwhelming majority of studies dealt with quantitative methods or macroeconomic or other issues not specifically connected to fundamental research and analysis. Few articles and books focused on the actual practice of analyzing companies and their securities or the craft of forecasting earnings and dividends from fundamental data and insights. Another interesting result of the literature search was that the popular press has increasingly focused on "superstar" portfolio managers with terrific (and typically short-term) records, and on highly visible Wall Street analysts; it rarely mentions the less glamorous buy-side fundamental analysts who work in money-management firms.

Throughout the literature on professional investing runs the sotto voce question of whether fundamental analysis actually makes any contribution at all. The efficient market hypothesis, depending on the strength with which it is argued, asserts that most of the kind of analysis I am talking about is a waste of time because everything that can be known about a stock is reflected in its price at all times. One rarely encounters real-life investors, however, who believe this thesis; many will hasten to provide numerous examples of stocks that soared or collapsed suddenly because of a new insight into their issuers' earnings or growth prospects. In fact, a counter hypothesis has recently been admirably formulated by Mordecai Kurz of Stanford University. This new theory, "rational belief equilibrium," argues that the price of a stock at any given time reflects the sum of all the forecasts that have been made regarding the issuing company. Kurz argues that most of these forecasts are wrong, in varying degrees, most of the time, even though they are rational in the sense that they are based on reasonable, but necessarily incomplete, evidence.

This new explanation of security prices is consoling to a research director and his or her analysts because it implies that they can find stocks for which the aggregate forecasts are more than a little wrong. If so, then they can add value to the investment process by identifying securities that sell for less than they are actually worth. The skilled analyst thus has a chance of gaining a competitive advantage by forecasting a change that is not already embedded in the price of a stock.

I am particularly pleased by this explanation because the first sentence in the description of the role of the equity analyst at Putnam Investments says that "the primary responsibility of the analyst is to anticipate the changes that will affect the prices and values of securities." (Kurz lives!) Occasionally, an analyst predicts a major, visible surprise. Obviously, a surprise is not a surprise if it has been anticipated, but that is a definitional quibble about a challenging pursuit that is not only fun but, when successful, can be extremely lucrative.

In any event, most "active" money managers, who work daily and often with great pressure and anxiety to find stocks that will outperform, do not spend much time thinking consciously about the rationality or efficiency of markets. They probably see these issues as imponderable matters suitable for metaphysical, quasi-epistemological, or theological disputes to be argued by others. Active professional investors get on with the daily challenge of managing both other people's money and their own businesses in an environment of consolidation and complexity.

Changes in the Analyst's Challenges and Responsibilities

As for the future, I think the increasing consolidation of assets among a fairly small number of managers will continue, for a variety of reasons. A primary stimulus is the drive for economies of scale that is increasingly dominating the mutual fund business and the defined-contribution retirement fund business, the fastest growing segment of the institutional industry. The result is that the world's largest money managers increasingly have the resources to assemble fairly large numbers of analysts, who struggle to create competitive performance advantages that are measured in basis points. I believe that this trend is already changing the role of the analyst from a fairly junior position on the ladder of professional success to a rewarding career path of its own.

Until recently, research analysts were typically entry-level employees right out of school who competed for higher paying and higher status jobs as portfolio managers. They were—and sometimes still are—mythologized as bright, solitary heroes who were supposed to pick the winners within large-coverage universes while avoiding the stocks that would decline in value. At the same time, they were at the beck and call of portfolio managers who had special requests and regarded the analyst's time and mind as resources to be commandeered at will. For many analysts, the job had much in common with juggling chain saws—a frenzied activity with a constant sense of terrible hazard and few satisfactions except the prospect of some day getting a "real job" as a portfolio manager. Rarely did an analyst have opportunities to do in-depth work on a circumscribed and realistic universe of companies, the kind of work that most in the profession believe leads to money-making recommendations.

A concurrent—and complicating—development was the rise of both "earnings management" and company "guidance" about expected levels of earnings. The focus of analysts, on Wall Street and in investing institutions, and of business reporters on the predictions of company managers created an environment in which analysts were not primarily concerned with creating independent opinions. Often, earnings estimation became a game of deciding whether management was trying to lower investors' expectations in order to create an earnings "surprise." Describing this game as analysis is difficult.

In the old model I am describing, an analyst who was still an analyst after five or ten years might feel career frustration, even though he or she was making a vital contribution to the investment process. Today, this view is changing. The analytical role in some of the big investing institutions is becoming a real and desirable career path of its own, with its own definitions of professional competence and its own rewards, status, and growth opportunities. Under the old model, a person worked for a few years as an analyst to train for a position as a portfolio manager; in the new model, a person has an opportunity to work a few years as an analyst in order to become a very good analyst. While the business still needs to train portfolio managers, analysts are not required to leave research in order to be promoted.

The new model for the analyst's role reflects the reality that the analytical undertaking is extremely complex. Not only is the competition among investment firms intense, but the investment environment is changing in ways that require extensive knowledge, skill, and cleverness in order to add value by superior analysis. For example, international earnings have become a critical variable in many U.S. companies. Last year, perhaps as much as 30–40 percent of operating income of U.S. companies came from non-U.S. operations. In fact, many, if not most, recent earnings surprises—both positive and negative—have been consequences of investors having inadequate insight into the foreign subsidiaries and operations of U.S. companies.

Corporate management is a particularly problematic source of information in this context. Its own information on overseas operations is frequently not up-to-date, and distance in geography and culture aggravate the natural human tendency not to tell the boss back home the bad news.

Another complicating factor is the proliferation of global stocks that can now be purchased in the form of American Depositary Receipt (ADR) packages. Growing numbers of ADRs are listed on the public exchanges, but the disclosure requirements often are not strict, so the kind of information needed to have a chance at anticipating meaningful changes is not as readily available in documentary form as it is for U.S. companies. Therefore, ADRs require the analyst to do more digging and to be literate in the use of foreign information sources and foreign accounting practices. Dealing with ADRs also often requires that the U.S.-based analyst have a foreign-based colleague with specialized skills and insights.

Another trend that is making the analytical challenge more difficult and more interesting than in the past is the multiplication of investment styles within money-management firms. Among the big firms, few continue to concentrate only on growth investing or value investing or international investing. This development means that analysts increasingly need to be skilled at researching and valuing both value and growth companies, in addition to bringing a global perspective to both styles.

Amid the increasing complexity of the world and the role of the analyst, a never-ending blizzard of Wall Street publications constantly threatens to bury the institutional investor. Last year, for example, five large brokerage houses alone generated more than 22,000 separate research reports. This deluge has two problems. First, the material itself is a mixed bag of some valuable and some low-value-added work. Finding the good in the midst of the chaff is difficult, especially for relatively inexperienced analysts. They may spend all their time culling "information" and little time transforming the information into the kind of knowledge that can lead to a clearly differentiated, profitable investment recommendation. Moreover, young or less-experienced analysts are more likely to be credulous than more experienced analysts because they have not necessarily learned that Wall Street does not get paid to make money for money managers.

Wall Street's economic interests have more to do with investment banking and security-trading fees than they do with making real money in real portfolios for real investors who have mortgages to pay and retirements to provide for. While this vested interest is no secret, it does add a dimension of difficulty to interpreting Wall Street's massive output. The bottom line, as they say, is that the new model of analytic professionalism emphasizes maturity of judgment and the development of a broad range of analytical skills, neither of which received thorough emphasis in the old model.

Yet another new trend is the widespread adoption of the "economic value-added" (EVA) approach to the management and the evaluation of companies. Briefly, EVA is a discipline that compares a company's cash-based financial returns to its cost of capital and tries to determine whether the company is creating or destroying value. The model can be a very useful management discipline, one that moves the focus away from reported accounting earnings and onto the real economic issues relating to the enrichment of shareholders. The rigor of an analysis of a company based on its EVA characteristics poses a new kind of challenge for analysts, however, who must create long-term models, usually at least five years into the future, in order to understand and quantify the economic value created by a company. This undertaking is not for a beginner; it requires not merely strong technical or academic skills but seasoned judgment and a realistic sense of the probable path of evolutionary change in a company. This sense usually comes with experience and is most likely found in a veteran analyst. (By the way, this kind of analysis is quite congenial to many analysts, including those at Putnam, who make detailed five-year models of the companies they recommend and use present-value methodologies based on discounting dividend and/or cash flows developed in the models.)

Finally, pressures on portfolio managers are also accelerating the professionalization of the analytical role. As investment products have multiplied and the dollar stakes have increased, particularly in various retirement categories, the requirements involved in maintaining relationships with clients—and the flow of information to them—have increased the demands on portfolio managers. Increasing client-service demands mean that portfolio managers have less time to perform their own research and are thus much more reliant on analysts than in the past. These changes on the portfolio-management side of the business are adding to the momentum for change in the analyst's traditional role.

Implications for Firm Management

The changes and complications inherent in redefining the analyst's role are putting stress on traditionally organized investment management firms. As the professionalization of research proceeds, the firms are creating circumstances in which the enhanced role of analysts is creatively accepted. The first, and probably most important, change is one that has so far taken place in only a few firms (among them, Putnam); this change is to make research a distinct career path. In firms making this change, an analyst does not need to become a portfolio manager in order to become a senior vice president or managing director or to enjoy compensation commensurate with that of portfolio managers.

Professionalization of research also requires a commitment by senior managers to creating world-class facilities for information research. These facilities may still be called "libraries," but they are not the old-style repositories of books and public documents. Now, because of computer power, libraries and professional research librarians can be sophisticated intermediaries of information in a variety of forms, increasingly electronic. The amount of well-organized information that a trained research librarian can uncover is tremendous. The library at Putnam, for example, has become a valuable research adjunct. We no longer keep paper files on most companies because we can access these documents either on-line or on laser discs. This ability means that librarians are available to do challenging research projects in collaboration with analysts. The library budget is not small, but its value far exceeds its cost.

Managing analysts as career professionals also poses a unique series of challenges from a psychological or behavioral perspective. "Professionalism" usually connotes some kind of rigid conformity to a batch of implicit or explicit guidelines and a belief that conformity to the profession's folkways and habits is good. People in the same profession tend to be like each other. They dress alike. They share jargon. They practice "middle-of-the-pack" behavior and often ostracize colleagues who drift to the fringes in matters of belief and opinion. Most of these characteristics of professionalism are exactly the behavior and thinking we do not want to encourage in analysts, for whom conformity is a kind of slow occupational strangulation.

Research managers in the new model need to help analysts resist the herd mentality, which has several million years of evolutionary force behind it. Resisting conformity at Putnam is an attempt to resist producing average analysis. Average analysis produces, at best, average stock selection, which leads to an investment standard that we consider too low. Putnam is finding ways to structure compensation policies and a departmental atmosphere that explicitly encourage attitudes and personal qualities that will produce superior research—qualities like imagination and curiosity. Mention of these qualities is infrequent in the literature of investing, but a few investors do advocate their cultivation. For example, Claude Rosenberg wrote in the early 1970s about some of the basic human questions one might ask about investors: How do you foster imagination? How do you keep curiosity alive? His book *Psycho-Cybernetics and the Stock Market* takes the very optimistic and, I think, constructive view that investors can actually encourage these virtues in themselves and, by implication, in others.[1]

A profoundly important point, in my opinion, is that managers of career analysts must recognize explicitly that the best analysts can be counted on to make mistakes some percentage of the time. Error rates are obvious through simple observation and are as universally true and powerful as the law of gravity. In the course of a career, even a great analyst or portfolio manager might be right only 60 percent of the time. I would argue, however, that the managers of investment professionals have traditionally made the implicit assumption that anything less than 100 percent "rightness" is unacceptable. This attitude is not only unrealistic, but it also makes errors appear to be exceptional events, not natural occurrences. The result is an atmosphere in which mistakes in judgment are not likely to be admitted and corrected promptly and freely. This issue is important because one of the most corrosive forces in organizations, in my opinion, is the fear of public humiliation, which leads to favoring inaction over risk taking.

At Putnam, we have devised an approach to errors or mistakes that, although unglamorous, seems to work pretty well. At the end of the year, we give special bonuses to the analysts who most creatively and in the face of greatest potential embarrassment changed their minds about an opinion that they had advocated. This approach takes a good bit of the potential humiliation out of changing one's mind and admitting error. In fact, after this plan was implemented, analysts quickly began to relax somewhat about reversing their opinions. I believe we catch our underperforming stocks earlier now and, therefore, are improving our relative performance numbers. This result should not be surprising, of course, because human nature tends to put off the admission of mistakes. The tendency is especially strong in the investment business, in which everybody, like all the children in Lake Wobegon, is supposed to be "above average." Even when something is probably wrong with an investment idea, analysts tend to say, "Let's wait for one more month of sales data" or "I'll make up my mind after I visit the company in a few weeks." We have all seen—and made—such rationalizations, which so easily lead to keeping underperforming stocks in portfolios too long.

An allied challenge for research managers is dealing with the high levels of anxiety and conflict inherent in this business. Every decision is made on necessarily incomplete information. A good invest-

ment decision requires that investment managers resist the tendency to reflexive conformity, which is setting the current price of a security. When a manager buys a security, she or he has decided that thousands of other very smart people have inadequate insight into it. In a big investment organization with huge assets, the result is frequent, if not constant, conflict.

I use the word "conflict" instead of "disagreement" because professional investors often are passionate about their convictions and conclusions and sometimes become completely identified with their opinions. This intensity is good when it brings great energy and focus to an investment process, but it also can accelerate the anxiety level in a business that already has huge uncertainties, and thus huge nervousness, built into it.

In fact, if a large investing organization has no conflict of opinions, something is probably wrong. Maybe everyone is being very polite and agreeing with one another in order to achieve consensus. Maybe one or two particularly negative and critical people are making their colleagues reluctant to express a variety of opinions in investment meetings. Neither scenario is conducive to achieving above-average investment returns.

The critical task for the managers of the investment process is to keep conflict and discord alive as a creative and clarifying force without letting it degenerate into morale-sapping fights. Success at this task depends more on the managers' and analysts' attitudes than on anything that can be built into a compensation or performance measurement system. Merely pointing out examples of successes built on strongly expressed differences of opinion can help a great deal because it assigns credit to the group rather than to the "victorious" individual whose opinion prevailed. Needless to say, this process requires managers to be comfortable with conflict and to see their roles explicitly as managing conflict rather than avoiding it.

Managing conflict is aided tremendously by the use of a consistent investment framework and approach. At Putnam, we have spent a great deal of time creating what we call common language and values, so that we have ways of talking about stocks in a consistent way that cuts across the traditional language of growth or value or international investing and gives us common ground for discussion and useful disagreement. We have found this approach to be useful because, although we have consistency in language and methodology, we are constantly aware of the potential conflict between creativity and conformity/consistency/control. Balancing and adjusting in order to maintain equilibrium and to avoid small-minded orthodoxy and niggling consistency is

[1]Claude Rosenberg, Jr., *Psycho-Cybernetics and the Stock Market* (Chicago, Ill: Playboy Press, 1971). See also Mr. Rosenberg's presentation on pp. 51–54.

management's constant challenge.

A similar balancing act is required if the analyst is to identify with the group but not practice "group think." The ideal analyst combines abstract thinking with ratlike cunning—ratlike because the job requires a ferreting out of useful information, resourcefulness, and tenacity that is anything but glamorous, and cunning because the analyst is trying to beat the competition in understanding trends and implications on the basis of too little information to make a definitive judgment.

An extension of managing conflict is encouraging collaboration, which is, in turn, an important part of fostering creativity. The old model of the solo analyst trying to outsmart everybody else on a stock does not work well in the modern investment world; there is simply too much for one person to know and evaluate. At Putnam, we try constantly to foster collaboration—not only among our equity analysts, but also among the large equity and fixed-income research groups. In most investing institutions, little interchange occurs between these two groups, but we have found that clear benefits come from constant collaboration. Our bond and stock analysts visit companies together and often work on their financial projections together, especially cash flow projections. One unexpected benefit has been that equity analysts have profited from understanding the distinctive perspective of high-yield-bond investors. These investors think like venture capitalists or owners of businesses, with few illusions about the safety net of market liquidity, and they work diligently on detailed "what-if" exercises to try to anticipate sources of possible surprises.

We have found that a good way to foster collaboration is to assign large problems to groups of analysts. If the problem is particularly thorny or involves an especially large investment position, two or three analysts are asked to drop what they are doing to attack it. The principles behind this kind of collaboration are simple: It can lead to faster problem solving, and people generally make each other smarter by bringing a sense of urgency and concentration to a group undertaking.

The premier analyst is one who excels at getting information, assessing it, putting it in perspective, and turning it into usable knowledge. The investment firm's challenge is to foster, simultaneously, the individual traits and the group identification that are both required for the process to succeed.

In addition, we believe that managing career analysts requires an emphasis on continuing education. Would you trust your brain to a neurosurgeon who has had no training since residency? Why should you trust your assets to a group of people who do not upgrade their skills on a regular basis? Several times a month, we hold research workshops led by specialists to give analysts fresh perspectives on accounting issues, changes in demographic trends, and a wide variety of other subjects.

The next big challenge for managers of creative investment professionals is to maintain a rigorous and daily enforced emphasis on forecasting. It is easy for security analysis to lapse into a focus on history—what used to be—which is interesting but insufficient for the task at hand. History is not destiny, it is a prologue to the future, which is the determining factor in securities valuation. At Putnam, we have tried to operate with disciplines that keep people thinking ahead and not confusing history with forecasting. At Putnam, our emphasis on rigorous financial models of the companies we own, for example, keeps analysts concentrated on determining five-year-forward normalized growth rates. We try to avoid the illusion of specious accuracy—for example, that we can predict a company's earnings five years in advance with a high degree of accuracy—but we can usually get a pretty good fix on the direction and magnitude of earnings growth. Moreover, the modeling discipline increases the probability of isolating and understanding the two or three critical variables that usually make the difference in a good purchase or sale recommendation.

A balance is also necessary between habitual knowledge and new understanding. People in this business often see in a current event some version of a similar event from earlier in their careers. This tendency can lead to terrible mistakes through confusing analogy with fact. As analysts accumulate decades of experience, the tricks for them are to avoid falling into stereotyped thinking and to be able to confront apparently familiar situations with a constant willingness to see change: "In the mind of the beginner there are many possibilities; in the mind of the expert there are few."[2]

Conclusion

The changes I have tried to identify in the role of the security analyst in large investment organizations are creating new opportunities for creative professionals to spend entire careers in research. Current trends pose real challenges to the managers of investment professionals. Although these challenges are daunting in many cases, meeting them will help analysts continue to add value to the investment process, to the betterment of the clients who rely on this profession to represent them in the capital markets.

[2]Shunryu Suzuki, *Zen Mind, Beginner's Mind* (New York: Weatherhill, September 1970).

An Approach to Growth Investing

J. Parker Hall III, CFA
President
Lincoln Capital Management Company

Do successful growth-oriented investment firms share common organizational and operating characteristics? Three determinants of success discussed here apply to all investment management firms; three other elements that are described—portfolio decision making, performance evaluation, and motivation—are intended to bring success in this firm's specific circumstances and given its goals and personalities.

Many investment firms focusing on growth stock investing have experienced remarkable increases in assets under management during the last 20 years. More importantly, evidence suggests that these firms did not sacrifice returns to achieve that asset growth; they matched or exceeded standard benchmark measures of performance. Do such firms share common organizational and operating characteristics? The intent of this presentation is to convey how one investment management firm implements growth stock investing. The first three aspects are characteristic of firms of all philosophical stripes: clear statement of philosophy, fit with client objectives, and research to support the philosophy. The next three aspects—portfolio decision making, performance evaluation, and motivation—are more specific to Lincoln Capital Management.

Philosophy

Whether an investment manager's philosophy emphasizes growth, value, or another style of investing is not important. But being able to make a clear statement of the investment philosophy is absolutely essential. Moreover, the manager should be able to say what the philosophy is in a sentence or two; doing so will help the manager focus on the philosophy and help clients understand the style.

One test a manager can make to define and sustain its philosophy is to examine the character of the 10–15 largest holdings in its client portfolios for each of the past five to ten years. Do the holdings reflect the philosophy espoused by the manager? Sometimes this test is not only instructive but also unpleasant, because a management firm may find that it is more flexible and less committed to the philosophy

than the firm believed was the case. A change in investment approach may be appropriate and defensible, but the manager should change the statement of philosophy to reflect changes in the character of actual portfolios.

Lincoln Capital Management's primary philosophical bent, for example, is to own stocks offering what many investors might consider moderate growth opportunities. The estimated future weighted-average annual earnings growth rate for the stocks in our client portfolios is about 14 percent. We are not "pedal to the metal," fast-growth investors.

Client Relationships

Many clients, particularly institutional sponsors and sophisticated individuals, prefer a manager that has a clearly defined philosophy—growth, value, diversified, or some other style. For example, 32 of Lincoln's current 35 equity clients hired us specifically for our growth philosophy. The remaining three equity clients hired us many years ago without a sensitivity to our philosophy.

When clients know what philosophy or style they want from managers, they are likely to be helpful, supportive, patient, and accepting of the periodic—sometimes multiyear—return shortfalls that all managers deliver. This understanding defuses the underlying tension that often exists between investment managers and clients and helps to lengthen the tenure of client–manager relationships.

One way to keep the investment management firm's character from changing too much over time is to limit the number of clients and to set relatively high investment account minimums. When the investment firm imposes meaningful constraints, the clients who do join are likely to be informed about the firm's philosophy and the firm can build assets at a rate that assures it can implement the philosophy effectively. Lincoln has a very high minimum threshold for new clients—since 1990, assets of $100 million—and, since about 1985, has limited new clients to one or two a year.

Research and Valuation

Most growth-oriented investment firms use an analyst-driven research approach that is grounded in intensive, bottom-up, fundamental analysis. One way of assessing a firm's capabilities in this area is to determine whether it hires only research analysts with extensive, documented, and productive experience.

Lincoln's ongoing equity universe contains approximately 220 stocks. This small size gives us an opportunity to concentrate our analytical attention on a limited number of fine growth companies.

For about 25 years, Lincoln has used a valuation discipline based on relative P/Es. For all the stocks in our universe, we try to relate current to historical valuations (all in forward estimates of earnings) of the stock, the industry, and companies of similar character. This analysis, together with what we know about the company today and how it may have changed, helps us establish a reasonable valuation goal. We are also at the early stage of doing some economic value analysis to help us in the valuation challenge.

Negative opinions of others play a role in our analyses, stimulating us to further research. This supplemental review may or may not lead to a different opinion about the stock, but we will be better informed for the effort.

Portfolio Decision Making

The three characteristics just described apply in varying degrees to most investment management firms. In decision making, however, Lincoln's approach is somewhat more distinctive. We want to attract and keep good research people—one of the biggest challenges for investment management firms—by motivating, stimulating, and engaging them to an unusual extent. One thing we have done is to give every analyst one full vote on every investment decision made by the firm, with the final decision reflecting the majority of votes. For example, a recommendation to buy a technology stock may come from an analyst who has thoroughly researched the company, but if a majority of the analysts who follow financial, health care, and consumer

nondurable stocks or industrials vote no, the technology stock will not be purchased. This approach requires all analysts to become informed about areas outside their specialties and to be truly objective, because they have effectively assumed the role of portfolio managers. A valuable by-product is that the potential exists for great loyalty to the firm and low employee turnover.

Lincoln implements portfolio decisions immediately, even during a meeting. Collegial decision making does not have to slow the process.

Reflecting its narrow investment philosophy and its decision-making process, Lincoln's equity portfolios are invested identically. An investment management firm that invests portfolios with similar styles and objectives differently lacks intellectual discipline. It is not giving each client the firm's best single portfolio. In addition to discipline, giving the client the firm's single best portfolio also eliminates the problems created when portfolio managers are compensated based on year-to-year results and clients receive wide-ranging returns.

Lincoln's portfolios are constructed with concentrated bets; our top ten holdings represent a relatively high 40–45 percent of the portfolio. We often buy or sell around those large positions as valuations change. Our diagnostics indicate these large holdings contribute positively to portfolio returns.

We tend to have fairly long-lived portfolio holdings with annual turnover a relatively low one-third. Turnover results not only from a response to deteriorating fundamental factors but also from sale of stocks that have met our valuation objectives.

Performance Evaluation

A style-oriented investor must have an appropriate style-oriented benchmark. Trends in the market favoring one style or another can continue for a number of years, and an inappropriate benchmark can be very misleading to the client in assessing performance.

The persistence of style-favoring trends is apparent in a comparison of returns for growth and value indexes. **Figure 1** shows the ratio of relative returns for the S&P Growth Index and the S&P Value Index. The ratio is set at 1.00 at year-end 1984; when the ratio is increasing and the line slopes upward, growth is outperforming value, and vice versa.

The first five years, 1985 through 1989, were basically a draw. In 1990 and 1991, a period of desultory corporate profits, the growth stocks exhibited highly superior performance. In 1992 and 1993, as corporate profits rebounded strongly, value stocks materially outperformed. Cumulatively for the ten-year period, growth outperformed value by about 1

Figure 1. S&P Growth Index versus S&P Value Index: Ratio of Cumulative Wealth Indexes

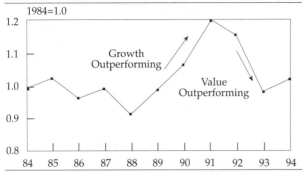

Source: Lincoln Capital Management.

percent.

Sponsors or investors focusing on either of these styles who did not recognize and understand these trends could have been easily misled about investment management performance. Managers have been hired and fired in the last few years because clients judged them to be smart or dumb when, in reality, both clients and managers were often simply using the wrong benchmarks.

The importance of using an appropriate benchmark is further illustrated in **Figure 2**. The graph depicts the performance of Lincoln's composite port-

Figure 2. Lincoln Composite Portfolio versus S&P–BARRA Growth Index: Ratio of Cumulative Wealth Indexes

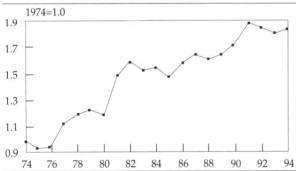

Source: Lincoln Capital Management.

folio (which is in compliance with the AIMR Performance Presentation Standards) in relation to the S&P Growth Index. The ratio of the Lincoln composite wealth index to the growth wealth index is set at 1.0 in 1974, the initiation of the S&P sector indexes. When the ratio is increasing and the line slopes upward, the Lincoln composite is outperforming the index, and vice versa.

For 5- and 10-year periods, Lincoln outperformed the index by about 2 percent a year, and for periods of 15 and 20 years, by about 3 percent. The figure shows numerous relative ups and downs for the composite, and in fact, the composite underper-

formed the index about 40 percent of the time. We regularly share with clients such public benchmark comparisons as those in Figures 1 and 2.

Lincoln's own customized growth benchmark, started in 1986, was the outgrowth of a futile search for an index appropriate to a seasoned growth stock investor. We have used this customized benchmark for about ten years—as well as the Russell 1000 Growth Index in recent years. Clients often have their own benchmarks that can be incorporated into analyses and used to illuminate comparisons.

Manager Motivation

The quantitative aspects of motivation revolve around compensation and ownership participation. Lincoln's approach to compensation is based on the premise that, despite the seemingly limitless range of diagnostics and attributions one can run on portfolios, relative returns—even adjusted for style—are essentially random for periods of one to three years. That is, the odds that an active portfolio will have consistent relative returns during short time periods are very small.

In this context, a long-term perspective on compensation is critical. Lincoln does not pay annual bonuses to investment people; if short-term performance is more or less random, annual awards are meaningless at best and, at worst, may be positively misleading. Paying for something that is random sends the wrong message. Similarly, we pay no flat salaries. Distributable earnings are a direct function of revenues and expenses, so compensation is directly related to how the firm as a whole is performing for its clients.

The long-term perspective, and long-term motivation, is further affirmed by the opportunity Lincoln managers have for equity participation in the firm. Lincoln is wholly owned by its investment professionals and top administrative officer. We thus have to satisfy only two constituencies—our clients and ourselves. The investment people have a direct interest in having the firm do well in the long run, and the firm will do well only if the clients do well.

Conclusion

Regardless of predominant investing style, an investment management firm's ultimate success will be determined by its ability to attract good people, articulate its investment philosophy, and create productive portfolios. Additional issues involve a coherent investment process (including in-depth research), valuation disciplines, participatory decision making, and the maintenance of similar portfolios. Performance benchmarks should be appropriate to the investment style and should be regularly shared with clients. Finally, motivation and incentive plans, particularly for compensation and ownership, should foster a long-term perspective that will benefit both the firm and, more importantly, its clients.

A Unique Approach to Growth Investment Management

James R. Jundt, CFA
Chairman and CEO
Jundt Associates

Successful growth investment firms share some ingredients; they have firmly held philosophies, operating structures that reflect those philosophies and the people in the firm, and consistent, disciplined implementation. The approach described here illustrates some uncommon aspects of the ingredients—a true team approach, dual large- and small-capitalization management, a focus on revenues and return on equity, and pursuit of companies run by the entrepreneurs of tomorrow, companies that will benefit from inevitable changes in society, and companies that are not dependent on the state of the economy.

Although many valid approaches to the stock market exist, Jundt Associates believes that the people and firms who have achieved good long-term results share some common characteristics. They have a philosophy they believe in; the philosophy is compatible with the personalities of the investment principals and the operating structure of the firm; and the implementation is consistent and disciplined on a long-term basis.

Operating Characteristics

Jundt Associates is a relatively small firm that has existed for about 14 years. When Jundt Associates was organized, we decided the company should have no more than 25 clients. The goal was to create a firm in which the investment personnel would spend the greatest amount of effort possible on the investment process and still have time to deal directly with the firm's clients.

One of the unique characteristics of our firm is that we operate on a team basis. Although many organizations claim to function as a team, our observation is that few do so to the degree Jundt Associates does. Some firms maintain a commonality of, say, 70 percent among the accounts but managers handle portfolios individually. At other firms, the term "team" is really synonymous for a committee process.

The four money managers at Jundt Associates do not manage portfolios individually. Before a stock is purchased, the sponsoring portfolio manager must present it to the team for discussion. Regardless of the opinion of his peers, once this process occurs, the money manager is free to implement the idea in each portfolio. At Jundt Associates, some of the best ideas are those that are championed by an individual manager although the others disagree. Once a manager's name is on a selection, the other three have a vested interest in the performance outcome of that stock. Thus, if the selected company does not perform according to expectations, the manager who made the purchase is under tremendous pressure to admit his mistake. Although this process involves some inherent conflict and stress, the continual questioning and critiquing of their selections sharpens the skills of all four managers.

Another aspect of the team approach is that Jundt Associates pays the four managers as principals, giving no further incentives that might undermine the common objective. This policy contrasts with that of firms in which individual achievement versus one's peers leads to promotions and/or bonuses.

A second unique characteristic of Jundt Associates is that managers individually manage both large-capitalization and small-capitalization portfolios. Many organizations in the United States manage large-cap/growth and small-cap/growth portfolios, but instances of the same individuals managing both types are rare. This characteristic is beneficial because it forces associates at Jundt to look at new and young companies—companies that are growth stocks—as well as established companies. Jundt's large-cap core portfolios benefit from this system because managers' familiarity with the small companies often results in these companies being added to core portfolios sooner than if we were investing only in large-cap companies.

Focus on Revenues

In contrast to most growth managers who emphasize "momentum investing" and, in particular "earnings momentum," Jundt Associates, for a number of reasons, focuses on revenues and return on equity (ROE). First, the simple laws of economics and finance dictate that, on a long-term basis, *no company's earnings can grow faster than its revenue stream and ROE*. Second, most businesses appear to be governed by a natural profit margin. In addition, portfolio managers are all aware that corporate managers today have too much discretion in defining what earnings are. In the short term, corporate executives can thus make earnings whatever they want them to be within fairly broad parameters, and the markets invariably overreact to the results of those earnings manipulations. For example, Jundt bought Microsoft stock on the initial public offering. Today, Microsoft stock is more than $100 a share, but at one time the stock was down 5 points, even though revenues were up more than 70 percent, because the company reported earnings gains a penny shy of some Wall Street estimates.

We sometimes buy into an earnings disappointment, but we never buy into revenue weakness. For example, we sold IBM at $150–$160 a share—not because we were smarter than the rest of Wall Street, but because IBM no longer met our minimum requirement for revenue growth. Since then, IBM has attributed its falling stock price, first, to a product transition and, next, to the state of the economy; excuses have abounded. The fact is that the world changed, and IBM's revenues stopped growing.

Buy Discipline

When we have identified a company as one of the 30–50 fastest growing companies in the United States, even if the price is 50, 60, or 70 times earnings, we buy a minimum position of 1 percent and implement it across all portfolios. Too often, money managers miss a great growth company because they spend time debating a good entry point. When Digital Equipment had sales of $25 million, it sold at 60–80 times earnings, but it became a $10 billion company. Invariably, Jundt portfolios exhibit some of the highest average P/E ratios in the industry, but we believe multiples will "take care of themselves" with adequate revenue growth.

We never buy more than a 3 percent position, and regardless of how successful a company becomes, we never let our position in it exceed 5 percent. The primary rationale for these rules is that we never want to put ourselves in a position where an individual decision will unduly influence the progress of the portfolio. The 1 percent minimum position, rather than 3 percent, is taken when the support for an idea is coming from only the one manager sponsoring the investment.

Focus on Genius

Jundt Associates attempts, within certain parameters, to own stock in 30–50 of the fastest growing companies in America. Rather than concentrate our efforts on attempting to buy low and sell high, we search for entrepreneurs and managements who can develop small companies into billion dollar firms. We focus on the genius of others, people like Sam Walton, Bill Gates, and Bernie Marcus. We emphasize management talent because we believe the markets are brutally efficient and that information today is a commodity; therefore, we do not attempt to prove our own genius by buying low and selling high.

Focus on Societal Changes

In addition to identifying corporate genius, we look for stocks of companies that will benefit by inevitable changes in society. We have done very well with growth companies that turn the luxuries of today into the necessities of tomorrow. For example, a few years ago, a cellular telephone cost $4,000. To purchase one for personal use was truly a luxury. Today, that same phone is free to customers who sign up for a specified period of service. When cellular technology was first developed, people were debating whether the market penetration would be 5 percent, 6 percent, or 7 percent. Jundt Associates thought penetration might someday be 70–80 percent, and we set out to buy the stocks in the forefront of what we considered to be a technological revolution.

Indeed, the universe of growth companies is changing dramatically. The growth companies of the past 20 years, with a few exceptions (such as Wal-Mart), are probably on their last legs as growth companies. Growth investing, however, is more exciting today than at any other time during my career. A typical Jundt core portfolio (defined in the "Portfolio Characteristics" section) today has 36 investments, of which 21 involve companies that were not in existence or were quite small as recently as 10 years ago. Microsoft is a prime example of the latter. Even for Wal-Mart, the sad day will come when we must sell it because of the law of large numbers: If Wal-Mart were to grow in the next 10 years as it has grown in the past 10, the company would have revenues of $400–$500 billion by 2005. This is not likely to occur.

Other Considerations

Somewhat ironically for a firm that does not believe in financial models, we also look at ROE to evaluate growth. On a long-term basis, no company can grow faster than its ROE. If it grows faster than its ROE, a company must do one of two things: leverage itself or dilute the existing shareholder base through the sale of additional stock. Neither development is good for the shareholder.

Finally, Jundt searches for companies that can increase their revenues independently of the state of the economy. The ideal investment is one that can go up whether Democrats or Republicans control the White House, whether inflation is rising or declining, and whether the economy is in a recession or a recovery.

Portfolio Characteristics

Jundt portfolios exhibit several characteristics common to those of many growth-oriented investors, along with some not so common facets in the areas of performance, composition, and construction rules.

Performance

The average annual corporate earnings of stocks in the Jundt core portfolio, on a composite basis, have grown tremendously—approximately 38 percent—from 1990 through 1994. **Table 1** compares stocks in the Jundt core portfolio with the S&P 500 Index. In the latest 12 months shown on the table, the average increase in earnings has accelerated to 55 percent.

The most critical factor however, is the average increase in sales for the latest quarter. Revenues on a composite basis were up 36 percent, versus 11 percent for the S&P 500. Table 1 also indicates the five-year average ROE to be 21 percent, roughly equal to our portfolio returns during the past 14 years.

Composition

The 38 percent revenue growth highlighted in Table 1 suggests a speculative portfolio; we would characterize the core portfolio as aggressive, certainly, but not speculative. For example, approximately 70 percent of the companies in the portfolio have revenues greater than $750 million.

Equity securities make up 94.6 percent of the core portfolio, with cash and cash equivalents making up the remainder. The portfolio's holdings are allocated to the following industries: 24.8 percent communications, 23.5 percent retailing, 14.9 percent computer services/software, 9.9 percent health care/medical devices, 5.6 percent electronics, 5.4 percent restaurants, 3.3 percent interactive media, 3.2 percent biotechnology, 1.0 percent computer

Table 1. Comparative Analysis: Jundt Core Portfolio versus S&P 500, December 31, 1994

Characteristic	Jundt Portfolio	S&P 500
Average size of companies owned		
Shares outstanding (millions)	215.25	169.51
Market value (millions)	$7,816	$6,660
Average daily volume for 50 days (shares)	655,667	398,124
Annual sales (millions)	$4,914	$8,232
Average P/E		
Latest 12-month earnings per share	35	18
Based on earnings estimates	31	17
Current yield	0.3%	2.7%
Average annual growth rate of earnings (5 years)	38.0	8.0
Average percent increase		
Latest 12-months' earnings	55.0	22.0
Latest quarterly earnings	44.0	25.0
Latest quarter sales	36.0	11.0
Percent of stocks with latest quarter earnings down	8.0	21.0
Percent of stocks over 200-day moving average	58.0	44.0
Average profit margin after tax (%)	7.2	7.1
Average return on equity (%)	21.0	15.4
Average alpha[a]	1.3	na
Average beta[b]	1.77×	1.06×

Note: S&P figures are unweighted. The Jundt portfolio owns 18 stocks traded on the NYSE and 18 traded over the counter.

[a]Monthly percentage return during past five years (without general market influence).
[b]Volatility relative to general market.

na = not applicable.

Source: Jundt Associates, based on data from William O'Neil & Co.

equipment, and 3.0 percent miscellaneous.

Devoting one-quarter of the portfolio to cellular communications stems from our belief that the United States is in the midst of a wireless communications and personal computer revolution that will continue for many years. The downfall of IBM was caused by the rise of the personal computer. Ten years ago, IBM said the personal computer was a toy, and at the time, IBM was right. IBM, however, did not recognize that the power of that toy would increase by a factor of two every 18 months. We believe, for example, that Intel will develop a computer in 12–15 years that will cost $5,000 and have the power of today's Cray.

The health care companies comprise a much smaller position in the portfolio today than they have historically. Moreover, four of the five investments are health maintenance organizations (HMOs), which we believe will be beneficiaries of the major emphasis on cost containment in health care and of the aging of the population. HMOs' revenues are growing 25–100 percent annually.

In the retail area, we own the so-called category killer—those companies that lower gross margins to generate significantly greater revenues per store than their competitors. We do not own the stock of department stores, whose business has become ex-tremely competitive. For example, 25 years ago, one could buy a Ralph Lauren Polo shirt only at an up-scale department store; today, the shirts are available at half a dozen stores. Achieving above-average financial returns is difficult when six or seven major competitors are also selling the same product, with color being the only differentiation.

Construction Rules

In constructing our portfolios, we never violate certain disciplines under any circumstance. As noted previously, we always buy a 1 percent position in companies identified as appropriate and we follow the 3 percent and 5 percent rules. Our sell discipline consists partly of this 5 percent rule and partly of the discipline that when revenues fall short—not earnings, but revenues—we sell. Decisions to buy stocks are generally based on rational factors, which is why almost all managers are good buyers. Decisions to sell stocks involve emotional factors, which is why most managers are poor sellers. In addition to the explicit sell discipline, we believe the team approach encourages rational selling because there are always three managers playing the devil's advocate role to the sponsoring manager.

Growth Stock Investing Today

Claude N. Rosenberg, Jr.
Principal
RCM Capital Management

During the past 40 years, growth stock investing has involved being in the right place at the right time and being patient in the face of unfavorable developments. Can growth stock investors rely on past practices in the future? Certain principles of growth investing seem to be timeless, but changes in the investment environment are making the identification of growth stocks harder than in the past and producing changes in several attitudes and practices of growth stock investors—from the definition of earnings momentum to analyzing pricing strategy to the location of tomorrow's entrepreneurs.

Growth stock managers benefited enormously from the change that took place in common stock investing when investors switched from emphasizing yield to emphasizing total returns. For most of the 60 years prior to the time I entered the securities industry in the mid-1950s, common stocks provided investors higher current yields than bonds. Soon, however, investors began emphasizing growth in asset values in addition to yield. For growth stock investors, this change was fortuitous, and most will admit that they were lucky; the recognition of growth stocks came at the right time.

This expanded perspective, along with an upward progression of stock prices, also meant that growth stock investors had many years in which they could be very patient, perhaps even complacent, with many of the stocks in their portfolios. Turnover could be very low, and benign neglect served many clients and investment managers well.

Occasionally, however, events disturbed this otherwise pastoral scene. The Nifty Fifty fad in 1971 and 1972, for example, pressured wise investors to sell growth stocks because they were so overpriced. In 1975 and 1976, growth stock investors worried as analysts insisted that pricing power had shifted to the hands of commodity companies, so traditional growth stocks would disappear. Growth stock investors lived through the 1980s era of leveraged buyouts taking center stage in the stock market and the concurrent neglect of the most successful companies in favor of companies that were generally less efficient and simply ripe to be acquired. The year 1991 brought a new set of worries. Branded consumer products were threatened by generic and private-label compe-

tition, health care entities faced serious price competition, and other once secure, "protected" companies faced not only reduced growth prospects but even deteriorating profits.

The questions now are: Can growth stock investors in the future rely on past practices, and where are the growth stocks of today and tomorrow?

This presentation discusses the basic principles of growth stock investing, first addressing several characteristics that appear to be timeless in nature, then considering factors that may change to varying degrees over time. The presentation closes with a summary of elements that will be important to the success of growth stock investing in the foreseeable future.

Characteristics of Growth Stock Investing

Although other investing styles have sometimes done better than growth stock investing during the past 30 years or so, in general, growth investors have experienced consistent and often superior success. Many of the basic characteristics of growth stock investing are as relevant today as they were in the past; other tenets of the growth approach, however, have changed and may require modified strategies in the modern investment climate.

Timeless Characteristics

Growth stock investing is grounded in several historical principles that are still valid today.

■ *Turnover ratios.* Based at least partly on an understanding that market timing is folly and will not produce consistent returns, growth stock investors in the past kept turnover ratios low. No contemporary evidence exists to argue the efficacy of market timing, so low turnover is still an advantage favoring growth investing.

■ *Total returns.* A total return perspective suggests that the rate of return from growth stocks can (and should) be higher than the historical rate of return for common stocks in general. Growth investing has produced higher returns than returns from cyclical stocks experiencing no growth; the growth style also contains advantages over investing in most stable companies, which possess little or no growth potential and provide medium dividend yields.

The higher potential return from growth stocks has a fairly simple explanation. If an investor chooses companies with growth and, on average, is reasonably correct about the growth rate, then with merely a constant earnings multiple, the growth will produce capital appreciation for the investor even without high dividend yield. That is, if a company is growing at 15 percent and the multiple remains the same, an investor in that company might experience an approximate 15 percent increase in its market price over time—especially if increasing dividends accompany advances in earnings per share (EPS).

■ *P/Es.* Whereas many growth stocks already sell at premium prices, a portfolio filled with accepted growth stocks entails high risk of disappointment. Practicing humility with some recognized growth stocks makes sense. The well-known growth stocks ought to be balanced with companies that are not widely accepted but promise more rapid earnings increases than the recognized growth stocks. Sooner or later, the P/Es of the faster growing companies will probably rise, and the investor will benefit from the double-barreled effect of elevated EPS and P/E—a bonanza. The hunt for this effect naturally requires foresight; it motivates growth stock investors to be creative and imaginative in their analyses of companies. For example, Waste Management's first market exposure was simply as a garbage company, but far-sighted growth stock investors projected that it might become a successful "environmental" company. At one time, Motorola was simply a television, radio, and semiconductor maker, but canny analysts foresaw different trends in technology and could project that Motorola's P/E would go up with a stronger and less cyclical growth pattern.

■ *Noncyclicality.* Many growth stocks are international corporations and thus are somewhat insulated from any one national economic cycle. Other growth stocks are companies with diverse businesses and markets, so they also are relatively less affected by cycles.

■ *Macroeconomics.* Many of the choice growth companies of the past were the beneficiaries of moderate to high inflation; ironically, those companies were to a great extent responsible for that inflation because they wielded unusual pricing power in their particular industries. Moreover, most of those industries had substantial barriers to entry; in contrast to the contemporary scene, particularly in technology, few so-called garage businesses developed to sufficient maturity to challenge the established growth companies.

One irony in the consideration of these historical factors is that most growth stock investors considered themselves value managers who were simply looking farther ahead than investors with other styles and were willing to wait longer for results. Growth stock investors who bought companies at very low P/Es, such as Johnson & Johnson at 9 or 10 times earnings, were in fact combining the epitome of value investing with attractive growth characteristics.

■ *Taxes.* For most of the past 30 years, investors could easily see that the ordinary income tax rate was higher than the capital gains tax rate, sometimes substantially so. In the context of that differential tax treatment, growth stocks provided definite advantages to taxable investors. That favorable differential exists today, and changes in the political landscape may even enhance the capital gains tax advantage.

Changing Characteristics

Not all tenets of growth stock investing remain totally valid in their original forms; some attitudes and practices, reflecting the evolution and complexity of the investment environment, have changed or are in a state of flux.

■ *Cyclicals.* Cyclicals involve a special decision process for growth stock investors today. First, most cyclicals represent relatively mature industries, with low unit growth potential. Second, the most productive selection process for cyclicals is to buy them at the highest P/Es (when their profits are depressed) and sell them at the lowest P/Es (at peak periods that will be followed by declining profits).

Current conditions are likely to confuse growth investors. Even without a surging economy, many cyclical companies are much farther ahead of the growth companies in the evolving American business climate of cost cutting, operating efficiencies, and favorable profit leverage. To regain their attractiveness, many growth companies will need to emulate the recent habits and characteristics of the cyclicals.

■ *Dividends.* Attitudes toward dividends are changing. Growth stock investors always thought one of the reasons to own growing companies was that dividends would go up rapidly, which would compensate for the low yields at the beginning. Returns on cost would grow steadily, and in time, yield would be very high. Commencing in the late 1980s, however, many companies that would have traditionally raised dividends repurchased their own shares instead; hence, growth stock investors may have to look to appreciation to carry more of the total return burden. If the companies selected are solid, however, and they make repurchases propitiously, total returns to the investors should become attractive over time.

■ *People.* A basic tenet of my growth stock investing has been to invest in companies with the best people as opposed to those with the best current product. This tenet is even more important today than in the past because the life expectancy of products is continually decreasing. The flexibility and creativity required to overcome product obsolescence are more important than ever. But the tenet is becoming harder and harder to follow.

Growth stock investors typically have believed that their companies have the best managers in the world: After all, how many of the top business school graduates from 1950 to 1970 went into "heavy" industry? Not many. That situation has changed, however; management talent is now distributed more evenly across all sectors of the economy. In fact, many cyclical companies adjusted to modern techniques and greater efficiencies earlier and more astutely than those that headed the growth industries of the 1980s. It is not too late to catch up—and the better companies are well into implementing the necessary changes—but the onus is on growth investors to separate those who are adjusting properly from those who are clinging to the past.

■ *Pricing.* Many growth companies of the past few decades benefited enormously from the pricing power that was inherent in providing differentiated, branded products. Many had the ability to control markets, to raise prices consistently, and to increase margins along the way. Many corporate managers and growth stock investors "got fat" because of the luxury of such pricing power; many failed to take into account that premium pricing will not work with less differentiated, commodity-like products. The best companies have balanced internal cost reductions with more competitive pricing. They are regaining market shares and protecting their futures. In many cases, they are sacrificing near-term growth in exchange for eventual dominance.

■ *The growth culture.* Corporate cultures play a factor in whether companies can be defined as growth companies, but making that differentiation is harder to do today than in the past. For instance, Johnson & Johnson consists of 160 separate companies, each with its own entrepreneurial approach that serves as an impetus for growth. In contrast, growth investors have to question whether compa-

nies forced to shift from government-type work to open-market commercial competition can make the proper people and culture changes.

■ *Global factors.* Many of the companies growth stock investors own have large global businesses and must deal with the fact that currency exchange rates pose a greater risk today than in the past. Analysts must conduct a thorough and careful evaluation to determine whether a company is truly competitive or whether it only seems competitive because the dollar is cheap.

The rise of the emerging countries as investment opportunities has introduced another element of analysis. Growth stock investors can simply buy an emerging country index on the theory that the whole emerging market qualifies as a growth entity. Investors may find, however, that the growth companies in a particular nation, the least mature entities, would be termed cyclicals in the United States. For instance, a cement company may be a growth company in China or India. Not that Coca-Cola and other consumer product companies that have operated abroad for a long time cannot be growth companies, but in the emerging markets, growth stock analysts may have to adjust their habits to take into account companies not traditionally thought to be "growth" companies in America.

■ *Earnings momentum.* Growth stock analysts have always been greatly influenced by earnings momentum, but the definition has changed. Those involved in the growth style used earnings momentum data either to discover or to confirm continuing growth prospects.

The use of earnings momentum, however, has been taken to an extreme. Today, earnings momentum is short-term oriented, and in many cases, people are basing decisions on this momentum alone, caring little what business a company is in or how good it is. That extreme use of earnings momentum has become similar to charting.

The theory behind charting in the beginning was that the charts reflected the beliefs of people who best knew the fundamentals of the stocks or had the special information about what was happening in various companies. The theory was reasonably sound; an investor could examine a stock's chart and perhaps spot what the knowledgeable people were doing. The fallacy of charting is that the more popular it becomes, the less the charts reflect the beliefs of knowledgeable people; instead, they mainly reflect what other chartists are doing.

Decision making based on earnings momentum has attracted many chartists who care little about the businesses represented by their stocks. Too many are playing "follow the leader." Too many assume they will prosper because of the "there is always a greater fool" theory, which is not the way big money has been made in the stock market.

■ *Book values*. Despite all the quantitative work done, a major decision rule in growth stock investing has been to create portfolios with high price-to-book ratios. The problem this rule creates is that it follows an era of the biggest corporate asset write-offs in history. Book values have obviously decreased substantially, and many consultants' growth lists include companies that would never be considered growth companies on a qualitative basis. Growth stock investing as a strategy must transcend such perfunctory decision rules.

■ *Return on equity*. Years ago, analysts generally expected growth companies to be the only entities enjoying high returns on equity (ROE). Wise investors did not want returns to become so astronomical that they attracted excessive competition, but they liked the fat margins that they assumed would be compounded as a result of the high ROE and concurrent reinvestment of cash.

Today, many companies are doing best by consciously limiting their ROEs and profit margins. Their managers recognize that high returns invite competition (again, because products are more difficult to differentiate and so easy to duplicate today). A recent example is a company in the San Francisco area that is holding to 12 percent margins rather than its competitors' 18–20 percent margins. The chairman of the company argues that his shareholders will be better served by keeping margins low today and investing in the company's future than by taking the short-term gains and subjecting the company to potential increases in competition. In short, some growth companies will not necessarily have the highest ROEs or margins; hence, investors, analysts, and portfolio managers have an additional challenge in identifying true growth companies.

Summary and Conclusions

The true growth company of tomorrow is likely to be recognizable by three characteristics today. First, it must be able to control its own destiny rather than be at the mercy of GDP. Second, a true growth company should be able to create future products that will be in demand regardless of currency levels. Third, a true growth company will have managers who can find the proper balance in pricing of products or services. That balance will establish price levels low enough to stifle dangerous new competition but high enough to produce sufficient (and growing) free cash flow to

strengthen the balance sheet and raise EPS and dividends over the years.

The best preparation for analyzing and investing in growth companies remains careful fundamental research. Not being dependent on Wall Street is important. Although the Street can provide useful information, analysts and investors need to incorporate sensitivity to what is going on in the field—in the commercial marketplace.

As always, analysts should be wary of what company managers tell them and be confident enough to ask the right questions. The interviewing process is extremely important, and too many analysts are in awe of interviewing/interrogating high company officials. The best approach in such discussions is to be prepared. Analysts should ready six of their toughest, most troubling questions about the industry or the company and insist on appropriate answers. If the managers avoid answering the tough questions, analysts can skeptically draw their own conclusions.

Financial and security analysts of the future will emphasize cash flow. Free-cash-flow figures should be confirmed by balance sheet analysis.

Investors should constantly remind themselves that growth industries of the past are not necessarily growth industries of the future; they are commodities. Analysts should always keep in mind the history of railroads, steel, automobiles, and so forth. Growth stock investors perhaps need more warnings than they think. They benefited from numerous periods in which they could be fairly complacent. Today, they must be conscious of myriad, rapid changes taking place in the United States and throughout the world—the increase of free trade, for example.

Despite these warnings, trying to be too precise in the valuation of good growth companies is normally a mistake. Determining the exact P/E a good growth company deserves is less important than assessing carefully how well that company is developing a future for itself. Of course, some P/Es will be extreme, but no magic number exists; no one can say unequivocally that 20 times earnings is "too high."

A growth investing strategy that is based on trust in the economy and its markets may lead to complacency. Such growth stock investors run the risk of developing hubris, and hubris leads to arrogance and pig-headedness. Hubristic people usually fail. Flexibility is the key. Growth stock investors who work hard to find good companies, exercise a bit of humility, and are content with reasonable valuation levels will be well rewarded.

Growth Investing: Earnings Momentum and Delivered Growth

Warren E. Shaw, CFA
Chief Executive Officer and Chief Investment Officer
Chancellor Capital Management, Inc.

Successful execution of growth stock investing today may be more difficult than at any time in the past 20 years. Success requires a core investment philosophy, the processes to implement it, and the ability to organize seemingly limitless quantities of information about possible investments. The quest is for above-average, long-term, delivered growth; achieving it requires pursuing critical company traits and applying the lessons to be learned from empirical evidence.

Executing a value-adding growth stock investing approach may be more difficult in today's environment than at any time in the past 20 years. This presentation examines the three major elements of successful execution of such an approach. First, successful execution reflects certain central convictions about investment philosophy and process. Second, the myriad sources of information and the quantity of information available today must be organized in a way that will add value in terms of portfolio returns. Third, research findings suggest that successful investing in growth companies requires focusing on what is really important and adds value.

Central Convictions

Successful growth stock investing is based on a few strongly held convictions about both the philosophy of growth stock investing and the investment process.

Philosophy

First and foremost, any investment philosophy must be simple, clearly defined, and focused. Problems inevitably arise if it is so complicated that managers cannot explain it to themselves, to clients, or to consultants.

A growth-oriented philosophy should focus basically on one issue: the growth stock manager's belief about how to add value in terms of managing portfolios. Three critical elements determine success in adding value by investing in growing companies. The first is securing long-term growth—capturing delivered growth on a long-term basis from the companies selected by the growth manager. This concept may sound simplistic, but at any given time, many companies may be expected to be growing at above-average rates when, in fact, they will not. So, the first task of any growth stock manager is to discriminate between companies that are expected to grow and those that will actually deliver growth.

The second element of a value-adding growth investment philosophy is the concept of momentum. Earnings momentum is an adjunct to capturing delivered growth, and as will be discussed, it can be enormously valuable in enhancing returns in a growth stock portfolio.

The third value-adding element, valuation, is important primarily as an additional source of information about the stock, particularly when a stock is very expensive. The investor does not want to overpay; doing so is likely to offset the excess return associated with capturing above-average delivered growth. Valuation should not drive the entire process, however. The primary considerations are securing long-term growth and making sure the near-term fundamentals are positive; cheap growth stocks are often cheap for good reasons.

In addition to these key elements, two critical value-adding underpinnings should accompany any philosophy of growth stock investing. As will be discussed later, research that is anticipatory and nonconsensus in orientation and quantitative techniques that go beyond traditional approaches have both demonstrated their power and ability to add value in the past decade.

Process

Once the philosophy has been articulated, the investment process needs to match that philosophy point by point. If the philosophy is appropriate, the process must be designed to execute it in order to produce the hoped-for alpha. For example, the portfolio structure may be built on the concept of identifying a normal portfolio with normal positions for industry exposures. These normal positions, with appropriate ranges around them, provide a useful context from which the manager can make decisions designed to add value.

Academics and practitioners recognize that control of trading costs is important if returns are to be optimized. How the manager trades and executes can subtract or add hundreds of basis points to returns, but the indexes against which results are typically measured do not incorporate any costs associated with trading. Therefore, seeking to minimize the total trading costs, including implementation, opportunity, and commission expense, is important.

Most investors think naturally in terms of return, but risk is equally important. Return optimization assumes generating a return at an appropriate level of risk. The way risk is monitored and controlled in growth portfolios, therefore, is critical to the delivery of expected performance. Risk may be controlled by closely analyzing common factor attributes relative to the benchmark. These attributes include size, quality, momentum, relative industry exposure, and tracking error.

Compliance is an important element of the investment process and one that clients should appreciate. Effective compliance management ensures that the process is executed in a manner that is consistent, uniform across all accounts with a common benchmark, and reflective of individual client restrictions. Compliance ensures the integrity of the process.

Organizing Information

Even the best philosophy of growth stock investing and the best processes to implement it can be frustrated by the blizzard of information to which modern investors and managers are subjected. Organizing this information in some usable form is thus a vital element of successful investing. The first step is to distinguish between forecast-based and fact-based data. In addition, the roles played by portfolio managers and investment committees must be understood.

Forecast-Based Research Analysis

Generally, in growth investing, traditional research analysis is oriented toward forecasting—trying to anticipate the future. The past is examined, but the growth analyst spends more time focusing on the trends and events that will shape corporate growth prospects. This type of research can be performed in house or sought from external sources such as brokerage houses.

In-house research, if available, should focus on the following areas:

▪ *Forming industry perspectives*. Clearly, identification of attractive growth industries with improving business momentum is vital.

▪ *Developing nonconsensus views*. Consensus expectations are already reflected in stock prices to a large extent, and the consensus is typically not correct. Therefore, nonconsensus expectations are critical in identifying value-adding stocks.

▪ *Ranking stocks*. A ranking methodology that reflects the results of in-house research is often useful. Such a methodology allows the growth stock investor to quantify what analysts are recommending and may improve the ways in which the investment managers apply analysts' recommendations in the investment process.

▪ *Forecasting fundamentals*. A forecast of fundamentals—including earnings growth rates, normalized earnings levels, and dividend payout rates—is important because these inputs enable the investment manager to use a standard dividend discount model. The DDM output, in turn, is a useful supplement to other commonly used valuation approaches that focus on absolute and relative ratios of price to earnings and, to a lesser extent, price to book value.

▪ *Providing valuation insights*. In-house analysts can provide important supplementary valuation insights because DDM models do not work uniformly well for all industry groups and for all stocks. For example, in the case of cable and cellular stocks, earnings and dividend estimates are more difficult to make and less meaningful than cash flow in valuing the stocks.

Brokerage sources of information can make several contributions to the investor's information base. The primary benefit is in providing broader and deeper company and industry perspectives than could be generated in house. A second benefit is in identifying the consensus view, which serves as a sort of benchmark for the growth investor's own expectations; the investment manager may well decide to behave counter to that consensus, but having the benchmark is an important piece of information. The third benefit of brokerage information is its contribution to the mosaic of economic, industry, and company information the investment managers are building from the numerous sources, both formal and informal, that can be found on the Street.

Fact-Based Quantitative Research

In addition to traditional, forecast-based research, quantitative stock selection (QSS) research is quite valuable from a modeling perspective. Quantitative analysis tends to be grounded in facts gleaned from the present and the recent past, from which the models project the future. Chancellor Capital Management's experience is that QSS tends to have a low correlation with forecast-based research in terms of identifying good stocks because QSS focuses on identifying favorable trends that will extend into the future whereas analysts often seek to identify inflection points for investment. The combination of the two approaches can produce a particularly useful information set.

Quantitative approaches have several aspects. One is to rank stocks on the basis of earnings momentum, either in terms of earnings surprise, earnings revision, or earnings acceleration. Another is to provide a risk perspective by measuring the historical quality and stability of earnings results around a trend line. Quantitative approaches also tend to rely on relative strength as a measure. This element has not worked as well for growth stock investing as the earnings momentum measure, but it can add some value to the analysis.

The Portfolio Manager's Role

Perhaps the most important contribution of the portfolio manager to the effective management of portfolios is an unwavering focus on the client's risk–return objective and any associated constraints. In addition, portfolio managers provide top-down perspectives to the process, such as investment themes, strategy, and tactics. For example, the manager can make sure that the structure of the portfolio exhibits exposures appropriate to the benchmark, that the portfolio strategy reflects a long-term (one to three years) horizon, and that the short-term tactics being used are consistent with that strategic view. Implementation, trading costs, and compliance also all clearly fall into the portfolio manager's purview in terms of how to structure and process information flows.

The Investment Committee's Role

Committees provide guidelines for investment processes and portfolio structure. They can also be of benefit by setting objectives for each of the organization's equity products and by establishing investment policy, normal positions, and relevant operating ranges. Committees may have difficulty generating nonconsensus perspectives, however, because they tend to generate consensus thinking.

Research Findings and Lessons for Growth Investing

Chancellor Capital Management has carried out extensive research on the characteristics of successful growth stocks. That research has reinforced some of our essential convictions regarding growth investing and uncovered several other concepts that seem to add value to the process.

Delivered Growth

One of the critical questions facing growth stock investors is whether growth underperforms value as a style. Numerous studies indicate that the value style outperforms, but the problem is that the studies are not truly studying value versus growth. They are measuring what might be termed high-expectation and low-expectation stocks.

The low-expectation stocks tend to be the undervalued securities that may be found in a value stock portfolio. On the other side of the ledger are the high-expectation stocks. This universe does not necessarily represent high growth, and it certainly does not represent high *delivered* rates of growth. High-expectation stocks fall into two categories: those that deliver above-average growth and those that do not. What underperforms value investing is the composite, the performance of which is stunted by the stocks that do not actually deliver superior growth rates over the long term.

The key for growth investors, therefore, is to invest in the high-expectation subset that will deliver above-average growth. **Figure 1** illustrates the potential returns from such a strategy. The Russell 1000 Growth Index serves as a reasonable proxy for the selection universe of growth stocks for the time period. In Figure 1, the stocks in this universe were organized by rate of delivered growth into deciles from highest to lowest for each year. The figure shows what return investors would have received if they had invested in the top three deciles (an expo-

Figure 1. Delivered Growth: Compounded Return of Top Three Deciles within Russell 1000 Growth Universe

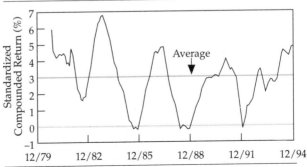

Source: Frank Russell Co.

sure of about 1 standard deviation) of a rolling real-time universe of large-capitalization/growth stocks delivering above-average growth, measured annually. In the 1980s, the top three deciles contained companies such as Wal-Mart, Home Depot, and Toys "R" Us. The average annual return premium generated by focusing on these kinds of companies would have been 300 basis points. The companies in the top three deciles were high-expectation stocks. They produced dramatically superior performance not because they were cheap and not because investors were surprised on the upside but because they simply delivered above-average growth in line with expectations.

Of course, the big challenge is to identify with perfect foresight which companies will deliver the superior growth. In fact, some interesting work has been done that allows investors to identify the kinds of companies that will produce above-average delivered growth. **Figure 2** compares earnings revisions with delivered growth in the Russell 1000 Growth

Figure 2. Correlation of Earnings Revisions and Delivered Growth within Russell 1000 Growth Universe

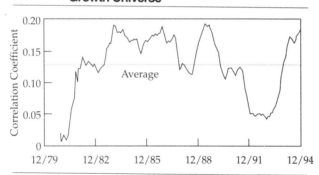

Source: Frank Russell Co.

Index universe. The figure takes historical earnings revisions during three-month periods and compares them on a rolling basis with the rates of delivered growth realized in the subsequent 12 months. The graph suggests that a fairly strong relationship exists between companies that produce positive earnings revisions and those that produce above-average delivered growth in subsequent time periods. The relationship is high, strong, and stable enough to add significant value in discriminating between those companies that will grow at above-average rates and those that will not. A correlation coefficient of 0.12 is sufficient to add several hundred basis points of value a year relative to the benchmark.

Earnings Revisions and Momentum

In addition to the reliable prediction of delivered growth, focusing on earnings revisions provides in-

formation that adds significant value to the investment process. Research evidence from Chancellor and elsewhere indicates that, over the long term, companies that have above-average earnings revisions will generate superior returns. **Figure 3** shows that a 600-basis-point excess annual return is associated with maintaining a 1-standard-deviation exposure to companies with positive earnings revisions.

Figure 3. Earnings Revisions and Subsequent Returns within Russell 1000 Growth Universe

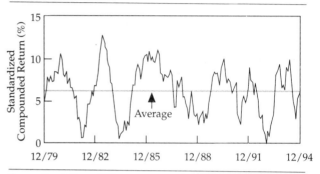

Source: Frank Russell Co.

Earnings revisions, in general, are an often overlooked anomaly in the market. Investors are generally unable to forecast earnings accurately, primarily because they follow the herd and the herd is typically wrong. They do not recognize that earnings revisions are serially correlated; that is, past changes in earnings estimates provide powerful clues to the direction of earnings surprises in the future. So, past changes provide clues to future estimate changes, and future estimate changes drive security prices.

Investing on the basis of earnings momentum is a strategy that has been discussed and analyzed thoroughly in the 1980s and early 1990s; so, one current question is whether this widespread attention and discussion has worked to decrease the strategy's validity. **Figure 4** examines this possibility by focusing on the last six years of returns. The figure presents an

Figure 4. Value Added by Earnings Revisions within Russell 1000 Growth Universe

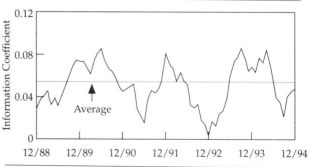

Source: Frank Russell Co.

information coefficient (vertical axis) that is the ranked correlation between earnings revisions and returns generated in the subsequent 12-month period. The trend in the information coefficient is flat, on average, during this period, which suggests that the ability of this approach to add value in growth investing has not been reduced. Investors are aware of and talking about earnings momentum but apparently are not using it aggressively and systematically. If they were, the slope of the line would be negative.

Another interesting observation about earnings momentum is that market capitalization within the growth universe makes a difference. **Figure 5** partitions the Russell 1000 Growth Index into two subsec-

Figure 5. Earnings Revisions and Returns by Market Capitalization within Russell 1000 Growth Universe

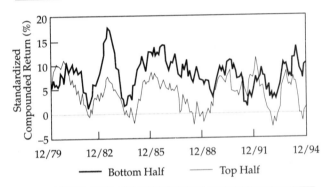

Source: Frank Russell Co.

tors; the upper half contains the 500 largest companies in the index, and the lower half contains the 500 smallest companies. The lines show that using earnings revisions as a stock selection indicator fairly consistently produces higher subsequent returns

among the smaller companies in the growth universe than it does among the larger. The strategy works across the growth universe but appears to be most useful when investing in medium and small companies.

Chancellor has also carried out research on the value added by earnings revisions in value investing as well as growth investing and found that earnings momentum works better when applied to a growth universe. So, our conclusion is that an earnings revisions strategy can add substantial value in the growth sector in general and in the small- and mid-cap growth subsectors in particular.

Figure 6 shows the results of applying a strategy based on earnings revisions to the retail subindex of the Russell 1000 Growth Index. For the most part during the six-year period, the strategy worked well in discriminating among and selecting retail stocks that added significant value in terms of subsequent return. **Figure 7** shows a similar approach for the health care subindex; in only one brief period in the last six years did earnings revisions not work well in selecting health care stocks that would subsequently produce substantial outperformance. **Figure 8** illustrates similar results for the consumer staples subindex of growth companies, which consists of food, beverage, and tobacco stocks. Earnings revisions have consistently predicted consumer staples stocks that will deliver superior returns, and that predictive ability has been particularly strong recently. The results for the information processing subindex in **Figure 9** are more complicated than in the previous examples because the subindex includes groups of stocks with different characteristics—hardware, software, and services, for example. Focusing on earnings revisions worked well throughout the period until the last six quarters; we do not know why this approach recently has not added value.

Figure 6. Earnings Revisions and Returns in the Retail Subsegment within Russell 1000 Growth Universe

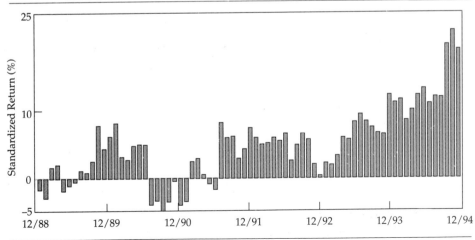

Source: Frank Russell Co.

Figure 7. Earnings Revisions and Returns in the Health Care Subsegment within Russell 1000 Growth Universe

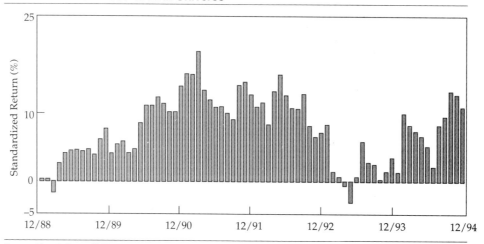

Source: Frank Russell Co.

Figure 8. Earnings Revisions and Returns in the Consumer Staples Subsegment within Russell 1000 Growth Universe

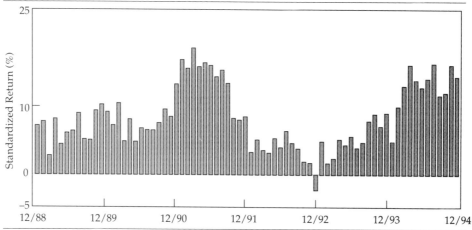

Source: Frank Russell Co.

Figure 9. Earnings Revisions and Returns in the Information Processing Subsegment within Russell 1000 Growth Universe

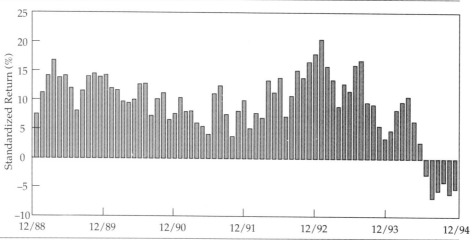

Source: Frank Russell Co.

Conclusion

The first and most important lesson about investing in growth is the necessity of capturing above-average, long-term, delivered growth rates. This goal is most likely to be accomplished by insisting that critical company traits be present in each investment idea—expanding markets, an outstanding franchise, outstanding management, high unit growth, and improving (or at least stable) profit margins. Investors able to find companies that fit this profile can use a "coffee can" approach to investing—essentially, parking their investments in these long-term gems and enjoying the benefits for five years or more.

Two problems mar this idyllic approach. First, very few growth companies have all the desirable growth traits at a given point in time. Second, a portfolio consisting of companies with those traits is not likely to be properly diversified. Therefore, most growth investors will need to supplement this approach.

That supplement can be achieved by maintaining an exposure to positive earnings revisions among growth investments. This approach has proved to be valuable in two respects. First, focusing on earnings revisions helps identify the companies that will deliver above-average rates of growth over the long term. Second, the strategy helps investors identify the growth stocks most likely to produce above-average performance in the short term.

Question and Answer Session: Growth

J. Parker Hall III, CFA
James R. Jundt, CFA
Claude N. Rosenberg, Jr.
Warren E. Shaw, CFA

Question: You suggested that the assessments of the key people in a company are an important part of your investment decision making. What have you learned about assessing and evaluating people?

Rosenberg: Certainly homework is required to determine just how hard people are working at the job. In the general geographical area where a company has its major presence, an analyst can investigate whether key company leaders are paying attention, are motivated, are exhibiting the flexibility needed in changing environments. Individuals, like companies, have cycles in their lives when they are accumulative and others when they are distributive. Knowing whether corporate leaders are still in an accumulative mode—not just accumulative in capital terms but also in terms of the "fire in their bellies"—is critical to the growth-stock-investing process. Nothing prevents analysts or portfolio managers from asking the tough questions necessary to find out.

Question: If you believe in a philosophy very deeply and those around you share that belief, do you run the risk of tunnel vision? How do you protect yourself and your firm from being profoundly wrong?

Jundt: One reason we have strict disciplines—never buying more than 3 percent at cost, never holding more than 5 percent—is to avoid those very problems. The disciplines reflect our judgment, based on experience, that "group thinking" is a danger; we have no single person responsible for a particular sector, and we do not want a single person designated "the expert" in a particular area. People often acquiesce uncritically to the perceived experts; that error is often the beginning of group thinking and group-endorsed mistakes. Most of our big mistakes have occurred when we all agreed 100 percent on a decision; we want people to be professionally critical of one another at all times.

Question: Please discuss one or two of your most successful investments.

Shaw: The prototype example would be Wal-Mart in the 1980s, in which we took large positions early. The important lessons there were quality and expertise of management and the commitment to pursue a consistent approach. The result was the delivery of dramatically superior, multiyear earnings growth. The key variables were not the cheapness of the stock or the consistent upward surprises in earnings revisions; the critical variable was a roughly 31 percent compounded earnings growth over ten years that translated directly into stock performance.

Another position we have held long term is Motorola, a company with management committed to the concept of excellence in their products. Motorola will benefit for at least another decade from the broad changes occurring in the economy and from the secular forces at work as the "wireless society" evolves.

Question: What did you learn from one of your biggest investment "blunders"?

Hall: We have probably lost money at one time or another on every one of the 200 stocks in our universe, so the modest blunders are numerous. One of our learning experiences with timing occurred in the mid-1970s. The 1973–74 bear market took stocks down 50 percent, and some aggressive indexes collapsed by as much as 90 percent. Fearing a repeat performance, we held relatively high reserves of 10–15 percent for the remainder of the decade. In hindsight, we clearly overreacted to the relatively remote prospect of another "bath."

Order Form 049

Additional copies of *Value and Growth Styles in Equity Investing* (and other publications listed on page 64) are available for purchase. Simply complete this form and return it via mail or fax to:

PBD, Inc.
P.O. Box 6996
Alpharetta, GA 30239-6996
U.S.A.
Telephone: 800/789-AIMR • 404/442-8631 • Fax: 404/442-9742

Name _____

Company _____

Address _____

_____ Suite/Floor _____

City _____

State _____ ZIP _____ Country _____

Daytime Telephone _____

Title of Publication	Price	Qty.	Total
_____	_____	_____	_____
_____	_____	_____	_____
_____	_____	_____	_____

Discount	$— _____
8.25% sales tax (New York residents)	$ _____
7% GST (Canada residents, #124134602)	$ _____
6% sales tax (Georgia residents)	$ _____
Shipping/handling	$ _____
Total cost of order	$ _____

SHIPPING/HANDLING CHARGES: Included in price of book for all U.S. orders. Surface delivery to Canada and Mexico, add $12 if value of books purchased is less than $50, or 18% of the total if value is between $50 and $100. Priority (air) delivery to Canada and Mexico, add $25 if value of books is less than $50, or 33% of the total if value is between $50 and $100. Other international purchasers should call or fax PBD for a shipping quote.

DISCOUNTS: Students, professors, and university libraries, 25%; CFA candidates (ID #_____), 25%; retired members (ID #_____), 25%; 50 or more copies of the same title, 40%.

❑ Check or money order enclosed payable to **PBD, Inc.**
Charge to: ❑ VISA   ❑ Mastercard   ❑ American Express   ❑ Discover

Card Number: ☐☐☐☐☐☐☐☐☐☐☐☐☐☐☐☐

Signature:_____ Expiration date: _____

Selected Publications*

AIMR

Corporate Financial Decision Making and Equity Analysis, 1995 . . . . $30
  Randall S. Billingsley, CFA, *Editor*

Credit Analysis of Nontraditional Debt Securities, 1995 . . . . $30
  Ashwinpaul C. Sondhi, *Editor*

Performance Evaluation, Benchmarks, and Attribution Analysis, 1995 . . . . $30
  Jan R. Squires, CFA, *Editor*

Real Estate Investing in the 1990s, 1995 . . . . $30
  Susan Hudson-Wilson, *Editor*

Fixed-Income Management: Techniques and Practices, 1994 . . . . $30
  Dwight D. Churchill, CFA, *Editor*

Blending Quantitative and Traditional Equity Analysis, 1994 . . . . $30
  H. Russell Fogler, *Editor*

Investment Policy, 1994 . . . . $30
  Jan R. Squires, CFA, *Editor*

Investing Worldwide V, 1994 . . . . $30

The Automotive Industry, 1994 . . . . $30
  Theodore Shasta, CFA, *Editor*

The Telecommunications Industry, 1994 . . . . $30
  Randall S. Billingsley, CFA, *Editor*

Good Ethics: The Essential Element of a Firm's Success, 1994 . . . . $30
  H. Kent Baker, CFA, *Editor*

Research Foundation

Bankruptcy Prediction Using Artificial Neural Systems, 1995 . . . . $20
  Robert E. Dorsey, Robert O. Edmister, and John D. Johnson

Time Diversification Revisited, 1995 . . . . $30
  William Reichenstein, CFA, and Dovalee Dorsett

Ethics in the Investment Profession: An International Survey, 1995 . . . . $20
  H. Kent Baker, CFA, E. Theodore Veit, CFA, and Michael R. Murphy, CFA

Corporate Governance and Firm Performance, 1994 . . . . $20
  Jonathan M. Karpoff, M. Wayne Marr, Jr., and Morris G. Danielson

Analysts' Earnings Forecast Accuracy in Japan and the United States, 1994 . . . . . . $20
  Robert M. Conroy, Robert S. Harris, and Young S. Park

Managed Futures and Their Role in Investment Portfolios, 1994 . . . . $30
  Don M. Chance, CFA

Franchise Value and the Price/Earnings Ratio, 1994 . . . . $30
  Martin L. Leibowitz and Stanley Kogelman

*A full catalog of publications is available from AIMR, P.O. Box 3668, Charlottesville, VA 22903; 804/980-3668; fax 804/980-9755.